How to Be a Woman Online

How to Be a Woman Online

Surviving Abuse and Harassment,
and How to Fight Back

Nina Jankowicz

BLOOMSBURY ACADEMIC
LONDON • NEW YORK • OXFORD • NEW DELHI • SYDNEY

BLOOMSBURY ACADEMIC
Bloomsbury Publishing Plc
50 Bedford Square, London, WC1B 3DP, UK
1385 Broadway, New York, NY 10018, USA
29 Earlsfort Terrace, Dublin 2, Ireland

BLOOMSBURY, BLOOMSBURY ACADEMIC and the Diana logo are trademarks
of Bloomsbury Publishing Plc

First published in Great Britain 2022
Reprinted in 2022 (twice)

Copyright © Nina Jankowicz, 2022

Nina Jankowicz has asserted her right under the Copyright, Designs
and Patents Act, 1988, to be identified as Author of this work.

For legal purposes the Acknowledgements on p. 87 constitute an
extension of this copyright page.

Cover design by Adriana Brioso

A catalogue record for this book is available from the British Library.

A catalog record for this book is available from the Library of Congress.

ISBN: PB: 978-1-3502-6757-2
       ePDF: 978-1-3502-6759-6
       eBook: 978-1-3502-6758-9

Typeset by RefineCatch Limited, Bungay, Suffolk
Printed and bound in Great Britain

To find out more about our authors and books visit www.bloomsbury.com
and sign up for our newsletters.

To Mom and Dad, for giving me the self-confidence and courage to dress as a bird princess and peck annoying little boys at the first grade Halloween Parade.

Contents

Introduction

It is a bright, cloudless morning as you leave for the office. You've been working your dream job for over a year, and you are just starting to feel like you're finding your stride: you know your employer's priorities, you feel comfortable in your role and your contributions to the organization, and you're not scared to talk about either of them on social media, a necessity for career advancement these days. You keep it real, too, posting the occasional snapshot from your daily life: a picture of your cat, perhaps a shot of your notebook, a pastry, and favorite order at the local coffee shop bathed in golden hour light, the ubiquitous post of every Instagram intellectual.

You're a few blocks from the metro station, thinking about your to-do list, when you notice a man following you at close range. You nod at him over your shoulder with a tight-lipped smile as he catches your eye. Feeling uneasy, you pick up your pace.

"OH, IS THAT HOW IT IS?" he shouts as you turn into the metro entrance. "ARE YOU TOO GOOD FOR ME OR SOMETHING? BITCH!" You try to shake it off as he keeps shouting. You reach the metro turnstile and take a deep breath as you make your way down to the platform. There's too much going on today to let this guy bother you.

Grabbing a seat on the next train, you settle in with today's newspaper. On the front page is an article in your area of expertise, the Russia-instigated war in Ukraine's east. The man next to you reads over your shoulder. "I went to Ukraine for a bachelor party once," he laughs, reminiscing and leaning in. "Hm," you barely reply, attempting to radiate unapproachability and shifting toward the window. "Beautiful women there," the man continues, undeterred. "It's a shame about the civil war, but this is probably the first time a young, pretty thing like you is hearing of it, I guess."

You gather your things and leave the car as he continues to mutter obscenities. Taking the steps on the escalator two at a time, you emerge into the daylight, likely looking harried, sweaty, and late, but you just want to put some distance between yourself and the guys you encountered on your commute. Rounding the corner onto your office building's block, a homeless man stands in an alley with his hand in his pants, pleasuring himself as he leers at you. In front of the entrance to your building, a group of people—mostly men—have gathered. Against all odds, the man who was following you and your fellow metro rider are there, leading the mob. Their cries pelt you from all angles.

"Tick tock! That's the sound of your biological clock ticking. Better go home and try to make a baby before it's too late, sweetheart."

"Check out the Adam's apple on you! You're probably a fucking tranny, aren't you?"

"Do you even have tits?"

"Learn the art of the blow job and make yourself useful for once in your fucking life!"

The security guard in the lobby doesn't seem to notice what's going on outside. Passersby keep their focus straight ahead and walk down the street as if nothing is happening. You were simply trying to get to work, and even if this angry crowd disappeared right now, the idea that you'd be able to concentrate, to write, to keep your cool in meetings and on phone calls, to banter with colleagues at the water cooler, is inconceivable. You are frozen, panic-stricken, and nauseous. You turn around and text your boss that you'll be working from home today.

*   *   *

The sentiments in the fictional scenario above are from my online admirers. As of this writing, none of them have been removed from the social media networks on which they were shared.

Most thinking, feeling individuals would be appalled to encounter a scene like this on the street. They would—we hope—intervene in some way. They'd offer to walk you into your building, accompany you home, or call the police. Law enforcement might make some arrests, or at the very least disperse the crowd. We expect such intervention in "real" life.

Online, however, that expectation doesn't exist. This type of abuse is the norm for many women engaged in public discourse, particularly those with marginalized identities. We accept that harassment of women is simply the cost of their social media engagement, or worse, that women are expected to endure harassment and silencing in the name of "free speech." It is long past time for that to change.

The first truly disturbing online abuse I received was in November 2018. I had been invited on the PBS *Newshour*, a no-frills, no-nonsense, nuance-filled nightly news magazine on America's public broadcaster. It was my third time on the program, and in a six-minute segment, I discussed my analysis of Facebook's ongoing self-regulation efforts. The segment aired on Thanksgiving Day.

The next morning, while nibbling some leftover cornbread, I sat at the kitchen table with my coffee, scrolling through my social media notifications. I had two Facebook messages in my "requests" folder— the place where notes from users who are not "friends" go. At 7:36PM on Thanksgiving night, when he might have otherwise been in a tryptophan coma or watching football with his family, a man named Brian located my account and wrote: *"I just watched your interview on PBS News Hour. I can't even recall what you were speaking of, because you said "UM" or "Uh" 16 times. Amazing anyone would interview you . . . I counted them . . ."*

Another guy, Edward Jr., seemed to have a similarly urgent message. *"Hello, Ms. Jankowics,"* he wrote, misspelling my last name, though he ostensibly had it right in front of him as he typed his missive, *"Hope you had a happy and blessed Thanksgiving. However,"*—however?!—*"I just watched your report on PBS* Newshour, *and I think I need to tell you I noticed something odd. While I was watching, I noticed the esophageal area of your throat seemed darkened. It may be the lighting, but I've seen many people in that situation who didn't have that appearance. It may be just your physique. Anyway, I don't mean to offend you in any way . . ."* I shared the message with some friends, who informed me that scrutinizing women's necks for evidence of an Adam's apple is a hobby of transphobic individuals looking for evidence that successful, attractive, headstrong women are secretly transgender.

I have never really been afraid of speaking up around men and boys; as a first grader, I pecked a little boy in the face while dressed up as a "bird princess" on Halloween. The costume was my own creation, merging the previous year's princess outfit with a bright pink bird mask, complete with a six-inch-long beak. Though I've always remembered that day proudly, likely thanks to my parents' bemusement and delight at my behavior, preserved forever on home video, it wasn't the triumphant day I now recall as an adult. My mom recently unearthed my first-grade journal, where that Halloween I wrote: "Today I am a bird . . . I am sad peple macke [sic] fun of me."

But I continued to do my best not to let anyone walk all over me. My mom fondly recalls a day more than a decade later when she overheard me on the phone, yelling at the male co-president of my high school's Debate Club for not shouldering his share of the work. I went to a women's college—Bryn Mawr, one of the Seven Sisters, a group of historic women's higher-ed institutions—an environment in which I was told my voice mattered. In my career, I've been lucky to work alongside inspiring women who have commiserated with and guided me, and to exist in a more equitable world than my mother or grandmothers had access to when they were my age.

But still, the relentless stream of online misogyny to which I and millions of other women who deign to engage in public discourse have been subject sometimes rattles me. I may have a slightly thicker skin than some, but watching thousands of strangers criticize my appearance, experience, and expertise is not easy. Watching them objectify me is not easy. Watching them deny me and other women our basic democratic and human rights is not easy. And watching these attacks be ignored as "the cost of doing business" in an age where an online presence is all-but-required is enraging.

This is where I tell you how troubling this problem is. I'm frustrated that this section needs to exist, but too many people—and as I found out the first time I was trolled, even some close to me—doubt the severity of online abuse. They doubt that it affects women more than men, and women from marginalized communities more than white, cisgender women. As MacArthur Fellow and legal scholar Danielle Citron writes in *Hate Crimes in Cyberspace*, many people trivialize online misogyny and harassment. They tell us to simply ignore the threats we receive. We are told women who report harassment are "drama queens" and the men who harass them are simply "frat boys" or sad men sitting in their underwear in their mothers' basements. We are blamed for wanting to equitably engage in the public sphere. (My trolls have told me more than once "if you can't take the heat, get out of the kitchen.") We are reminded that the internet, as the "virtual Wild West," has no rules, nor should we expect any to be enforced.[1] Sarah Jeong, a *New York Times* columnist, writes that the media also frequently mischaracterize the offline threats created by online abuse: "In the media narrative, harassment becomes unruly words, not Social Security numbers. It becomes rape threats, but not the publication of physical addresses. It becomes floods and floods of frightening tweets, not a SWAT team knocking on your door because someone on the internet called the police with a fake threat."[2]

None of these misconceptions should be acceptable in the twenty-first century. Here are some facts:

In the lead-up to the 2020 U.S. presidential election, the Institute for Strategic Dialogue found that women candidates for office were far more likely to be the target of abusive, often gender-based messages than their male counterparts. On Twitter, abusive messages comprised 15 percent of those women research subjects received, compared with only 5–10 percent for their male colleagues. "On Facebook, female Democrats received ten times more abusive comments than their male counterparts, while Republican women received twice as many abusive comments as Republican male peers."[3] The abuse was compounded for those women of intersectional backgrounds. Later in 2020, UNESCO and the International Center for Journalists (ICFJ) surveyed over 900 journalists from 125 countries, finding that 73 percent of women respondents had experienced online violence, including threats of physical and sexual violence. "Twenty percent … said they had been attacked or abused offline in connection with online violence they had experienced."[4]

In the same period, my research team at the Wilson Center embarked on a groundbreaking project analyzing the discourse surrounding 13 women politicians in autumn 2020. For two months, we collected mentions of candidates for office who spanned demographic and political divides across six social media platforms. As a women-dominated research team, we knew the conclusions would not be pretty; we were women with public online profiles, after all. But the sheer volume of the abuse, even outside of the nauseating content, was shocking. We uncovered over 336,000 pieces of gendered abuse and disinformation against our 13 research subjects, with 78 percent of instances targeting then-Senator Kamala Harris and her historic Vice Presidential campaign.[5] The tenor of the content was sexualized, racist or racialized, and transphobic in nature. Abusers claimed Harris had "slept her way to the top" or that her sexuality precluded her from government service, with nicknames like "Heels Up Harris" and "Cumala." They pasted Harris's face on pornographic images or on bodies in suggestive positions. In one breath, abusers employed racist stereotypes about Black women, and in the next they claimed "#KamalaAintBlack," alleging that Harris played up her African American roots to win votes. Unable to fathom a woman being successful without being duplicitous or exhibiting male characteristics, QAnon conspiracy theory supporters frequently shared a poorly Photoshopped meme that alleged Harris was secretly a transgender man named "Kamal Aroush." In all, similar gendered disinformation narratives affected nine of 13 research subjects, while 12 of 13 women in our sample were targeted with broader gendered abuse.

We by no means uncovered everything; online misogynists, we found, are expert at evading detection, using what I called "malign creativity." In the disinformation research sphere, we often call those that spread disinformation "malign actors." Here, they are using their creativity for malign purposes, employing coded language, iterative, context-based visual and textual memes, and other tactics to avoid scrutiny and consequences. For example, abusers name groups dedicated to harassing Alexandria Ocasio-Cortez innocuous titles like "AOC Memes and Tributes" and "AOC Fan Club." They use images rather than text to abuse their targets, and crop, animate, or edit them so that platforms have a more difficult time tracking them once they've been detected. They write "b!tch" instead of "bitch." In short, even as social media platforms attempt to address this abuse, the most prominent women in the world face an abusive onslaught that affects their likability, their image, their safety, and the democratic prospects for women the world over, each time they log on.

To be a woman online is an inherently dangerous act. The attacks we endure are meant to silence us. They are meant to encourage us to stay home in "traditional" women's roles and not engage in politics, journalism, activism, academia, or public life more broadly. As one of my trolls wrote, "you birth babies, we build bridges." (It is a ridiculous sentiment; among other examples, it was women who built London's Waterloo Bridge during the Second World War, though history tried to erase their contributions. And that's leaving aside the false equivalence between manual labor and childbirth, the physical pain of which I doubt this troll and others like him would be able to endure, not to mention the psychological toll motherhood takes on women in a world that undervalues our expected contributions to society.) However nonsensical, however baseless and uninformed, there is plenty of evidence that suggests these attacks change how women engage online.

In my own experience, I've found I think differently about how to promote my work when I'm actively dealing with abuse. Should I send a provocative tweet? Pursue research and publish writing on issues that attract criticism? Post a picture of myself online, giving the men obsessed with dissecting my appearance fodder for their next campaign? Sometimes, when I am engulfed by impostor syndrome or simply too tired to deal with another wave of online bile, the answer is no. But even in those moments, I know I'm not alone.

The International Women's Media Foundation found in a 2018 global survey that 40 percent of respondents "avoided reporting certain stories as a result of online harassment."[6] In 2019, the National Democratic Institute found that politically-active women sent fewer tweets in the aftermath of online abuse, experiencing a chilling effect.[7] An anonymous blogger, who "asked for her name not to be used because she was concerned about the attention that writing would attract" told journalist Helen Lewis in 2011, "the misogynistic abuse that a number of women bloggers and writers have received functions as a form of censorship and warning to the ones not currently experiencing it to watch what we say."[8] A leading disinformation researcher and personal friend told me in an interview for the Wilson Center's "Malign Creativity" report that when she is harassed, "oftentimes, my solution is to lock down my account ... or I completely go offline and I don't post for days.... You don't feel safe to continue speaking, so you don't speak."[9]

But what about young girls and women observing these campaigns? They may feel joy at the inauguration of Kamala Harris as the United States' first woman Vice President, but will they want to follow in her footsteps when they encounter the persistent disinformation campaign about her that scrutinizes her appearance, her race, her ethnicity, and her sexuality, all based on misogynist tropes?

In the course of my research, I ran focus groups with high school- and college-aged women, all of whom are extraordinarily careful with their online presence. "We know not to talk to everyone we meet. We're careful about what we post [because] we have seen people crash and burn because of the mistakes they've made," an 18-year-old from Chicago told me.[10] Her peers expressed worries about whether college admissions officers and future employers would pick apart their profiles. They were frightened that unsavory characters might discover where they lived or worked. Her college roommate, a 19-year-old from Virginia, said, "I don't want a lifestyle that public anymore."

It may seem admirable that these young women are taking precautions to keep themselves safe. They keep their Instagram profiles private, are wary on online dating sites, are careful when posting pictures of their faces and homes, and do not use their real names on social media profiles. While online vigilance is certainly warranted at times, I worry that young women today cut off a valuable avenue of self-expression and political and social engagement. They do not see the online world as it exists as one in which they can freely express themselves. As these young women transition into careers and an adult life that requires a public online presence, will they be at a disadvantage? Research suggests they might be. Plan International, a development organization that fights for the rights of girls, found that young women around the world are self-censoring in a frightening way. In their annual "State of the World's Girls" report in 2020, Plan asked 14,000 girls across 31 countries about their online habits. In a survey and interviews, they found that "most girls report their first experience of social media harassment between the ages of 14–16. Gradually, they learn to protect themselves better."[11] But that protection often amounts to self-censorship and can have psychological and other emotional offline effects. Some girls avoided going to school after they were harassed; young women had trouble finding employment. They sometimes feared for their physical safety and frequently changed their online behaviors. "Of the girls who have been harassed very frequently, 19 percent said they use . . . social media platform[s] less and 12 percent just stopped using [them]."[12] The authors trenchantly note that this sort of harassment should not be viewed through a "free speech" lens: "girls pay a high price for other people's, largely men's, 'right' to free speech. They are left to mostly cope on their own with a level of unremitting harassment that would see many of us defeated."[13]

Social media platforms are only just beginning to take these attacks and their downstream effects on democracy seriously. Governments, continuing their long history of failing women and systematizing misogyny, have by and large refused to see the urgency of these problems. Employers often do not have the systems in place to support the women representing them in the public sphere. Law enforcement are not equipped to handle online harassment, abuse, and disinformation, both in their training and background and the infrastructure of the legal system itself. Generally, women must navigate an often-treacherous online landscape and deal with the fallout themselves. Until platforms, governments, and employers actively begin to make the structural changes necessary to make the online environment more equitable, we need strategies to deal with online misogyny and to fight for a world that recognizes that our rights to free expression online are just as valuable as our abusers'. Right now, the onus is on women to manage these problems. It is not our fault that data brokers are selling details about our personal lives to anyone who will pay. It is not our fault that social media platforms cannot keep up with a malignantly creative trolling class that seeks to push women out of public life. It is not our fault that some male politicians tacitly endorse these behaviors, belittling their women counterparts and engaging in sexist tropes. It *is* infuriating, but there are ways to make it less so.

Enter this book. I have been extraordinarily lucky to have a network of women who have supported me through the online abuse I have experienced. I have also extensively researched the tactics and tools of online influence campaigns, including the myriad ways they are weaponized against women. Let's be clear: I do not have a foolproof strategy for dealing with online abuse, but I can teach you the practical strategies you need as you put yourself out there. They will not insulate you from abuse—to some degree, the abuse is a signal you're doing something right—but they'll keep you safer while it happens and remind you you're not alone.

Who is this book for? How many Twitter followers must you have accrued to make you care about this stuff? Do you need to go on TV regularly, or be a C-List celebrity, or an Instagram influencer? Zero, no, negatory, and nope. Online abuse, harassment, and disinformation can come for anyone at any time.

Do you identify as a woman? Then I regret to inform you that—just like you've probably been catcalled on the street while wearing your baggiest clothes on a day you feel like garbage—you will probably encounter online misogyny. If you work in a male-dominated industry like science, sports, or national security, you will see it in your Twitter replies, your email inbox, and the number of random men who quietly follow you on Instagram after a public appearance, unlikely to have done so to hear your political analysis. If you are a woman who is part of another ethnically, racially, or sexually marginalized group, you're even more likely to be targeted, and the attacks are likely to be more vicious. (Being a straight, cisgender, white woman, I personally cannot imagine what that is like; for more on the online experiences of women of color, follow Seyi Akiwowo, Shireen Mitchell, or Mutale Nkonde. If you are looking to understand the perspective of trans women in the public eye, look no further than Katelyn Burns.) While it is easy for those who haven't experienced online abuse to counsel a stiff upper lip, it is much harder for women to reconcile a barrage of personalized, violent physical threats with today's online surveillance technologies and the incessant fear of offline physical violence with which women contend on a daily basis.

This book is an attempt to give you a little more control. It is not meant to scare you, but to empower you to safely use your voice without regret or undue fear. Not every piece of advice that follows will be applicable for every one of you at every moment, but in reading on, you will fill up your online arsenal so you are ready to spring into action if the need arises, as well as preempt some of the more serious attacks, should they ever occur.

Most of all, this book is a call to action. By putting ourselves out there and asserting our rights to free online expression, women are slowly challenging the repulsive norms that allow online misogyny to continue to exist. If we demand solutions to the problems that social media platforms have yet to solve, if we draw attention to the fact that enduring abuse should not be the cost of being a woman on the internet, I have hope we can change the norms by which our online ecosystem is governed. I believe this book will help you do it.

I will introduce you to a few of the many women who inspire me as I take you through the basics of dealing with online harassment and abuse. You'll meet Cindy Otis, a former CIA analyst, counter-disinformation maven, author, and self-described "proud disabled woman" who has both been the subject of relentless abuse via QAnon conspiracists and other malign online communities *and* uncovered some truly frightening disinformation and influence campaigns through open source investigative techniques. The good news? We can reverse engineer some of those same techniques that allow Cindy to catch the bad guys to keep ourselves safe online.

Next, we'll meet Nicole Perlroth, a seasoned *New York Times* journalist who covers the extremely male, extremely toxic beat of cybersecurity, and Van Badham, a playwright, activist, and columnist for *The Guardian* Australia. Nicole discusses how her online engagement has changed as she has gained prominence on the cybersecurity beat, covering some of the most shocking stories of the past decade and releasing a popular book. Van tells us about her online maxims: "don't bomb the village," and "embrace blocktivism." She'll also give us tips about how to avoid trolls who have an "engagement boner." For now, she says, online harassment "is not a problem to be solved, it's an ongoing tension to be managed." With Nicole and Van's help, I'll walk you through the options you have when you're caught in the line of online fire, from naming and shaming to ignoring your trolls, and why these decisions are not one-size-fits-all.

Beyond your personal engagement (or lack thereof) with your abusers, social media platforms offer options—some more robust than others—to navigate abuse. We will meet Brianna Wu, one of the women targeted during an online harassment campaign in the video game industry known as Gamergate, widely regarded as the seminal event that heightened online misogyny as we know it today. Brianna advocates for knowing social media platforms' native tools and terms of service inside and out and making them work for you. I'll help you navigate these systems, walking you through the safety and reporting tools that are available, when and how to escalate when your reports aren't being heard, and the documentation you may want to keep in case you ever take your case to law enforcement.

We'll also discuss the importance of seeking and cultivating community. Online abuse is a lonely experience that makes you feel as if the world is against you. Worse, sometimes your closest friends and family don't recognize or understand what you're going through, further isolating you. If not for my support systems—some of which are made up of women I've never met in person—my experiences of online misogyny might have been much more damaging. We will discuss how to speak to your friends, family, and employer about what you're going through, and daily practices you can adopt to help create a more women-friendly online environment. Brittan Heller, a lawyer who was the Jane Doe in a landmark case of sexualized online abuse, gives us her perspective on building circles of solidarity—especially within the workplace—to support you during the most difficult times.

My greatest hope is that you will finish this book feeling empowered. Adopting these practices is not just about surviving online, it is about thriving, making your voice heard, and ensuring that our daughters can grow up feeling that they can express their opinions to exactly the same degree as the little boys they walk next to in the Halloween parade, no pecking necessary.

Security: Outfitting Yourself Online

I spent my formative years on the internet. For most of high school, my mother limited my computer usage to a half an hour a day, but that didn't stop me from publishing blogs on whatever the platform of the moment was. When Facebook opened to high school students, I was an early adopter. I posted photos from behind the scenes of musicals I was doing, and when I got to college, would complain about assignments, summer jobs, and the weather in my status updates and Facebook "Notes." I uploaded a regular stream of photos with what I considered witty captions from my on-campus escapades without much of a thought to them living in perpetuity on the internet or on anyone's hard drive who cared to download them. Relative strangers tagged me in photos when my band performed around the country.

I don't regret any of it. I had a great college experience, and compared with most American young adults' experiences at school, my time on campus was extraordinarily tame. There is no photographic or video evidence of me drinking heavily or using drugs because I never did. There are, however, a lot of less-than-flattering photos of me in my early college attire (sweatpants, t-shirt, and a messy bun), or acting like the enormous nerd that I was and am, singing with my college *a cappella* group, studying abroad in Russia, and playing concerts with my *Harry Potter*-themed band.

In 2020, a troll ran an ill-conceived smear campaign featuring videos of some of those escapades. He shared them on Twitter from an alternate account after I discussed disinformation in the presidential election. He tried to shame me into silence, but I wasn't ashamed. However, I was worried. This man had dug deep enough into my Google search results to find these videos. He selected the ones that made me look the least serious and professional, and went through the trouble of downloading, editing, and sharing them through an alternate account. If he found those, what else did he find? My phone number? My address? My mother's address? Would he ever deploy them if I debunked another one of his claims? Would I encounter him or one of his acolytes next time I walked the dog?

The night those videos were shared—the culmination of a week-long trolling campaign against me—my nerves and emotions were frayed. I felt unsafe and alone. I signed myself and my husband up for an anti-doxing service, which scrubs online white pages and other public records of your personal information for a fee. I had already been in the public eye for a few years, and so I took care with my physical and technical security, but that evening was a turning point in my online engagement. The days of posting my every fleeting thought or photographic evidence of the mundane occurrences in my life were already long gone, but now it was time for a new level of curation and caution.

*   *   *

Cindy Otis is one of the many women I've relied on to help me weather online attacks. She's a former CIA officer and fellow disinformation expert. Lest we forget that social media can be a positive place where friendships are formed, Cindy and I met on Twitter when we were both preparing to release our debut books. Since then, we've kept in touch through a steady stream of messages, celebrating our successes, lamenting days that could have gone better, and supporting each other through the worst the internet has to offer.

Just before the 2020 election, we were both called on to testify before the U.S. House of Representatives Permanent Select Committee on Intelligence, chaired by Representative Adam Schiff of California. The topic—"Misinformation, Conspiracy Theories, and 'Infodemics': Stopping the Spread Online"—couldn't have been more timely or more likely to attract the criticism of the very people who spread the malign information we were discussing.

The day before the hearing, "Q," the anonymous leader of the QAnon conspiracy cult, posted a message on 8kun about the proceedings. "Shall We show them, Anon..?" [sic] it began, before listing the names of the all-woman witness panel and closing with the phrase "Forewarned is Forearmed" and a salute to the "Q Team." The next day, Q adherents spent the two-hour hearing criticizing our appearances, making anti-Semitic slurs, and alleging we were all CIA plants. "Do we see a pattern here?" one poster asked, including a picture of the four women witnesses. "Look at the nose on that broad," a commenter wrote of me. Another implored, "show us your boobs!" Cindy, who is a wheelchair user and proud disability advocate, was grotesquely ridiculed. The discussion wasn't void of violent threats, either. One user wrote:

> *Find their feathers*
> *Light them up with truth!*
> *They have exposed themselves.*
> *Attack!*
> *This is a digital battlefield and we will not go silently.*

Cindy had already locked down her Twitter account. "I didn't need the stress of dealing with prep for [the hearing], executing that, and then coming back to disaster mentions" on Twitter, she tells me in a later conversation.[1] It's not a decision she takes lightly. "I know for a fact that that has caused me to [lose] opportunities to expand my reach and ... increase my credibility," she says. "When I lock down, nobody can share my content, nobody can follow me. There are those moments where you have that opportunity. I know I'm limiting my professional progress each time I scale back on social media. It's the calculation I make each time to prioritize my physical safety, my mental health."

As an open-source analyst and investigator who has uncovered disinformation networks that have made the pages of *The Washington Post* and other notable publications, Cindy is an expert on the digital breadcrumbs that can be used to target us. "Every social media user needs to make choices about how authentically themselves they're willing to be online," she underlines. The tidbits of our lives that make

us more human—our family issues, health issues, and personal stories—
"those can all be used to target you in the future, either by trolling or
through attempted recruitment by intelligence services," Cindy warns.
"The calculation might be that that's a vulnerability you're willing to put
out there, [but] you want to think carefully about the personal details
you're sharing that might put yourself in a more compromising
position."

But it's not just the personal details that can get you in trouble; basic
cyber hygiene is the foundation to any online security practice. No, it is
not the most exciting part of protecting yourself online, but it is the part
most connected to your physical safety. From password managers and
two-factor authentication to being savvy about the seemingly innocuous
tidbits you share on social media, you can build a moat around your
public profile, adding an extra layer of security and peace-of-mind as
you do your work and make yourself heard.

Basic Cyber Hygiene

Best practices to keep your data, profiles, and devices safe

In June 2021, Representative Mo Brooks, a Republican of Alabama,
tweeted a picture of his computer monitor. What was displayed on the
screen is unimportant compared to what was stuck to it: in the bottom
corner, a sticky note appeared to show Rep. Brooks's email password
and a PIN number. The tweet remained online for 20 hours before it
was replaced with a version with the sticky note cropped out.[2]

Women in the public eye do not have the luxury to be so careless,
nor could we possibly expect 20 hours of safety in such a scenario. If
Cindy or I had made a similar mistake around our testimonies, for
example, it's likely the QAnon cultists who dug through our online
profiles would have attempted to gain access to our accounts. They
wouldn't have been successful, because we follow the basic, easy
practices I'm about to outline for you that keep our personal information
safe from anyone who might try to harm us.

It's time to banish the sticky notes and scribbles at the back of your notebooks and proactively strengthen your online security.

Password managers

In today's digital world, we all maintain hundreds of passwords that are the first line of defense for our personal information. It is tiresome to try to read a news article or make an online purchase to be prompted for your username and password and guess blindly as to what they might be until you finally scrounge around in your desk drawer for the paper scrap that might hold the answer. Worse yet, perhaps you're in a rush, trying to buy a ticket to a popular concert, and are prompted to create a new account. Uninspired, you decide to make this password an ode to your dog. "ILoveFluffy," you type. The pet-less among us might go for a significant other's name, or worse yet, "password1234." And then, of course, there are the days you don't want to create a new password at all, and repeat your email or bank password, which you know by heart.

We've all been there, but this behavior needlessly exposes us to potential security breaches. If the concert ticket website is compromised, criminals now have access to the other accounts where you used the same password. This is entirely avoidable. It is extremely easy to set up a password manager, a service that will generate, store, and even input every password, username, and security question you have.

Here's how they work: after signing up for a password manager service (I use LastPass; other services include 1Password, BitWarden, and Dashlane), you create a single password that will log you into your password manager service. This is the *only* password you'll ever have to remember so long as you're using the service. From there, most password managers offer a browser plugin and mobile app that will store all the usernames and passwords for sites and services you use. You won't have to copy and paste them from site to site, and if you ever update your passwords, the service will log the change automatically. Most of these services will also identify weak or potentially breached passwords affected by large-scale hacks or leaks. A good password manager will also offer two-factor authentication to keep your accounts even more secure (more on this below) and ensure that if someone *did* crack your complex login information to your password manager, they would not be able to gain access to your account. (You should *absolutely* turn this on if it's available on the service you choose.) Best of all, when you create an account on a new site the first time, these services will generate a complex password, full of letters, numbers, and symbols, fitting the requirements of every site or service you use, and you'll never have to think of or remember one again.

Most web browsers and operating systems offer some version of a password manager (such as Apple Keychain or Google's Password Manager). Though they are aggressive, incessantly asking "Would you like to save your password?", convenient (pre-installed with your browser) and cost-effective (most of the best services on the market require a subscription fee of around $30 per year for full operability) they do not always offer the same features that an external service focused only on password management would.[3]

You may also be tempted to use single sign-on, employing your Google, Facebook, or Amazon account to log in to other websites rather than create new accounts. There are two reasons you should avoid this at all costs. First, the web titans providing those umbrella accounts are likely to harvest data about your behavior on third party services when you log in using the credentials from their site. More importantly, however, if your password for your Google, Facebook, or Amazon account were ever compromised, criminals could then access all your information on sites where you used them to log in. Yikes.

It is likely that you have been the victim of a password breach in the past decade. You can check this on the website HaveIBeenPwned.com (or its Facebook-centric sister, HaveIBeenZucked.com), which will run your email address or phone number against a database of known breaches. Since 2012, my own data—everything from usernames and passwords to my phone number and physical address—has been compromised 21 times. The website estimates that I belong to a cohort of over 11 *billion* other accounts. With services like LinkedIn and Adobe among those affected, you're probably in this frightening club, too. There's nothing you can do about the data that has already made its way into the world, but you *can* protect your accounts going forward, and the easiest way to do so is through a password manager. It's time to bid "ILoveFluffy" a tearful adieu. (You can keep your dog, though.)

Two-factor authentication

Suppose the worst happens: a social media platform you use daily is breached, exposing millions of passwords. Behind yours lies your personal information, private messages, and credit card information from the time you donated to your best friend's birthday fundraiser for Chengdu Panda Sanctuary. But you are savvy; you've enabled two-factor authentication on all your accounts, so criminals can't gain access. Your password manager alerts you to the breach; you change your password. Crisis—and the amplification of embarrassing messages to your college boyfriend by some troll in a dark basement—averted.

Two-factor authentication (sometimes abbreviated 2FA) plays a critical role in protecting you in this would-be worst-case scenario but is also helpful for protecting our digital selves more generally. Its basic premise is simple: in addition to providing your password to verify your identity and protect your data when logging into an online service (the first "factor" or token of authentication), it requires an additional confirmation that is delivered to you physically (the second "factor"). This can be in the form of a phone call, a text message, a code generated by a mobile app, or a physical security key that either communicates with your computer or phone via insertion or connects with them via Bluetooth. If a criminal were to try to gain access to your two-factor-protected account, he would input your stolen password and be challenged to use a second factor to confirm your identity. Unless you were—heaven forbid—kidnapped along with your two-factor device, most malign individuals would not be able to gain access to your accounts. Famously, John Podesta, Hillary Clinton's 2016 presidential campaign chair, did not have two-factor enabled when Russian hackers obtained his password through spearphishing and dumped the contents of his emails all over the internet at a key moment before Election Day.[4] Have I convinced you 2FA is important yet?

Enabling and using two-factor authentication is also comparatively easy for the protection it provides. This might seem highly technical, but I promise, it is accessible and incredibly important. Let's walk through the steps of setting it up on a third-party service like Twitter. You can usually find options to enable 2FA in the "security" section of a website, app, or service. When you reach this landing page on Twitter, you have three options for your second factor of security, ranging from least to most secure: a text message, an authentication app, or a physical security key. While texts are an incredibly easy way to get two-factor set up, and certainly better than no extra security at all, criminals can reroute text messages to their own phones and gain access to your account. I recommend that wherever possible you use one of the second two options—apps or physical keys—which take a little bit of preparation. You'll either need to download an authentication app (such as Duo Mobile, LastPass Authenticator, Authy, or Google or Microsoft's authenticators, for example), or purchase a security key from a company like YubiKey, which can run you anywhere from $25–70 per key.

You decide to add a security key to your Twitter account. You have already purchased it, so from here the process is smooth sailing. Twitter will ask for your password in a pop-up and then walk you through the steps of syncing your key to the account. You insert the key into your computer (or sync it on Bluetooth or near-field communication), touch it or press a button on the key, name the key, and you're done. The whole process takes about a minute. Twitter generates a backup code in case you lose access to your physical key, but you can now rest easy knowing your public brand is well-protected from whomever might seek to embarrass you online. (2FA alone is not a failsafe, however; malicious individuals can still gain access to your messages as they are being sent if you are on public WiFi and not using an encrypted messenger/email client, or virtual private network— a VPN—on which more later.)

I set up 2FA on literally every account I am able. Banks and hospitals often require 2FA, sending you a text code you input to gain access to their services. On some sites you will have to root around for the option, but it's worth it, especially for sensitive services like email, high-use social media platforms, or your password manager. For Gmail users who want a little extra peace of mind, Google offers the "Advanced Protection Program," which requires multi-factor authentication (a password and two other security keys) and provides a little extra support and monitoring from Google. (I am regularly notified that "state-sponsored hackers are attempting to gain access to my account, for instance. It's a little creepy, but I'd rather know that than be left in the dark.) If you would prefer to remain a target for online, economic, or physical attacks rather than input a code, acknowledge a pop up on your phone, or insert a USB stick, I can't help you.

Encrypted communications

In the vein of easy changes we can embrace to challenge those who wish us harm, anyone concerned about their online safety and privacy should take care with how they are communicating. I first started adjusting my online communication habits when I was living in Ukraine and traveling in other places known for state-sponsored digital surveillance. I wanted to keep my communications with my friends, family, and coworkers private and secure. But it's not just states that engage in digital surveillance; criminals, angry exes, and creeps do, too. Luckily, unless the person on the other end of your conversation is screenshotting or recording your interactions, it is simple to make sure your online communications are very secure.

You may already be using an encrypted messaging app such as WhatsApp. These apps are end-to-end encrypted, which means that before a message leaves your phone, it is translated into a complicated string of gibberish letters and numbers (a "cipher") that can only be decoded on the recipient's device. If you use an unencrypted messenger like Facebook Messenger or SMS (also known as text messages), if that service experiences a data breach or hack, the contents of all your private messages might be open to anyone who wants them. On end-to-end encrypted apps, no one except you can access your messages, including the messaging app itself and the government.

Encrypted messaging apps can still have vulnerabilities; WhatsApp and iMessage, for example, automatically back up users' chat logs to the cloud, meaning that your conversations and the media you exchanged on those apps are visible to anyone with access to your cloud storage account. You can turn off this feature in settings, but you will lose your chat history if you change devices. (In my opinion, this is a small price to pay in exchange for your privacy and peace of mind.) Telegram, another popular messaging app, has a different problem; its chats are not encrypted by default. Users must turn on this feature if they wish to preserve their privacy. Signal, an increasingly popular app initially developed for dissidents in authoritarian countries, is encrypted by default, does not back up your chat history, and has options to enable disappearing messages in individual chats. It is open-source, peer-reviewed, run by a non-profit, and free of the trackers and ads you might encounter on other apps, which is why so many people in unstable political situations rely on it to communicate.

Similar considerations apply to email; ProtonMail and several other providers offer end-to-end encrypted service, often for a monthly fee of a few dollars a month. Most mainstream providers, such as Gmail, are reading the emails you send and mining your conversations for patterns they use to sell targeted advertisements. While Gmail is decently secure (especially if you are using a password manager, multi-factor authentication, and enrolled in Google's Advanced Protection Program), users looking for an extra layer of privacy—such as journalists or those operating in countries where privacy is not guaranteed—should seek an end-to-end encrypted service.

On top of these adjustments, you should also consider using a virtual private network (VPN) client. VPN clients are apps (on your cell phone), plugins, or programs (on your desktop or laptop) that route your internet traffic to a secondary server in another location (sometimes another country entirely) before connecting you to the information you are seeking. All the while, your data is encrypted. VPNs aren't just for those dealing with uber-sensitive data; using a VPN blocks your internet service provider, your boss, governments, or creeps on public WiFi networks from seeing your online activity. Even if you feel you would be fine with your online browsing habits being made public, VPNs are a useful tool. VPN client TunnelBear describes the utility of their product this way:

> *Having nothing to hide and giving up your privacy are two very different things. Just because you're a law-abiding citizen, doesn't mean you'd keep your curtains open while you're changing. VPN protect your right to privacy from people that want to know your most intimate thoughts and personal moments.*[5]

There are many VPN clients on the market, but none of the best are free. Tech reviewers at CNET write: "Safe VPNs cost companies a lot of money to operate and keep secure, and free ones are almost always malware-laden data snoops."[6] Happily, most of the paid services offer free trials so you can find a service you like before making a commitment. As of mid-2021, CNET recommends ExpressVPN, Surfshark, NordVPN, ProtonVPN (created by the same engineers as ProtonMail), and IPVanish as the best VPNs.[7]

In short, using encrypted communications is not just for techies anymore; employing them is a relatively affordable investment that keeps you and your information more secure with few disruptions to your day-to-day life.

Anti-Doxing Services

It is frightening how much of our personal information is available online. Every day, online data brokers are crawling the internet to compile detailed profiles about us that they sell to anyone willing to pay. The profiles can include everything from your address, phone number, birthday, and Social Security number, to detailed demographic information, your preferred airline, health issues, and the type of roof on your house.[8] In addition to being unsettling and creepy, these services provide stalkers, trolls, and online armies an easy way to make your life a living hell through doxing, "the practice of publishing personal information about people without their consent."[9] As Sarah Jeong writes, "doxing can wreck your credit and leave you vulnerable to much more visceral threats, like letters and packages being sent to your home, or worse, assault."[10] Doxing can lead to "SWATing," when a fake emergency, like a hostage situation or bomb threat, is called into law enforcement. Police subsequently send a SWAT team to a target's house, putting them in a dangerous and potentially traumatic situation. Jeong underlines that "there is a clear and well-documented pattern of using doxing to punish women for being visible on the internet."[11] It's clearly not something most men need to worry about; when I asked my women Twitter followers to tell me about the inciting events that led them to sign up for anti-doxing services, several men replied something to the effect of "that's a thing?"

Luckily for us, they are. If you live in the United States, services like DeleteMe will do the dirty work of scrubbing your personal information from the web, for a fee. (Unfortunately, similar services do not yet exist for the British or European markets, partially because of the EU and UK's superior data privacy laws). Talia Lavin, a writer who has faced the online mob's worst elements, including neo-Nazis and white supremacists, says that subscribing to a service like this is her first piece of advice for anyone worried about being doxed. "Even if you are doxed now," she told journalist Lyz Lenz, using an anti-doxing service "makes it harder for them to find you in the future."[12]

These services are not cheap. You'll pay anywhere from $229–$999 *each year* to remove your information and that of one other member of your household (since a target's family members are often at risk as well) from the main online data brokers. If you can't afford the service, DeleteMe frequently runs promotional deals. I also recommend having a serious conversation with your employer about the necessity for a service like this for anyone—especially women, in particular women of intersectional identities—participating in public discourse. We'll discuss more about changing your employer's mindset in Chapter 5.

It *is* possible to file removal requests with all the individual data brokers yourself. DeleteMe publishes free guides to assist you in this project[13], which will take many precious hours of your life, as there are nearly 200 such sites online. In a world where the onus of dealing with online harassment and abuse is on targets, and you've already expended your time and emotion dealing with these ongoing campaigns, I feel that paying for safety is an extremely worthwhile investment.

Preserving your physical safety

You have a password manager set up. You use two-factor authentication. You keep most of your communications on an encrypted platform. You've preemptively signed up for an anti-doxing service. Surely now you've created an impervious internet fortress in which no one can touch you, right? Wrong. Even if your personal information is scrubbed from public records, the bad guys can still piece together a shocking amount of information about you, your habits, your home address, your favorite bar, and your friend group simply from analyzing your public online history.

"Anything that depicts a pattern of life puts you in a vulnerable position to someone who is going to choose targeted action," says Cindy Otis, the former CIA officer and author we met earlier. Seemingly innocuous information can be used to track your movements. If you share that you love getting tapas on Tuesdays with your girlfriends, you're putting yourself at risk.

Here's how that tidbit might play out with my own online profile: My author biography notes I live "outside of Washington, DC." I've tweeted information about coronavirus vaccines and elections in Arlington County, Virginia, so even a casual Twitter user can probably deduce that's where I live. Google reckons there are seven tapas restaurants in Arlington. If I shared a photo from my latest girls' night on Twitter or Instagram, it would be fairly easy for someone to analyze the surroundings and the food or drinks we ordered, cross reference that with the location, decor, and menu of Arlington's seven tapas places, and show up uninvited to my next girls' night. It's a scary thought. As Cindy notes, it's a constant calculation to decide how much of your life to share online. Here's what you should consider avoiding:

- **Real-time photos of your location.** Enjoying the summer sun in a local park? Wait until after you've left to share a photo, especially if you are tagging the location. Using the "close friends" feature on Instagram stories or creating a Facebook list containing people you know in real life and trust is a good way to scratch your sharing itch but keep yourself relatively safe in these situations. Some women may opt to completely lock down their personal social media accounts and restrict them only to people they've met in real life, not sharing any personal details in public fora.

- **Photos of or near your residence.** With the advent of Google StreetView, Google Earth, and other tools that have mapped and photographed our neighborhoods in extreme detail, seemingly innocuous snaps around the house can tip off the bad guys to your home address. The first time I lived in Ukraine, my apartment was directly behind the National Opera House. I once posted a picture of the Opera reflected in a glass of rosé I was drinking on my balcony. In those days, before I had a significant public profile, I was (perhaps naively) not as concerned about what the consequences of that photo might be. Today I would never post a similar photo. I'm also careful about pictures from my home and neighborhood where the street, neighbors' houses, or other landmarks are visible; they would be easy to geolocate. Even trees can give away clues about your location (especially when paired with the digital breadcrumbs about your tapas habit you've already dropped).

- **Photos of Fluffy or Fido with their tags visible.** Does your pet have an Instagram or TikTok account, or do you simply like to share photos of them because they're unbelievably cute? Make sure their tags with your address and phone number are either not visible, digitally removed, or best yet, turned to face inside so you can post with abandon. Similar geolocation caveats apply to sharing your pets' outdoor adventures, too.
- **Sharing tidbits about your life that might relate to account security.** If you "list your favorite city, your high school, or the make and model of your car," Cindy says, "you're basically providing the logins to your accounts and will be at risk of being compromised." If you *do* decide to share this information, think through whether it is connected to the security questions on any of your accounts.
- **Getting taken in by people you meet online, especially on dating apps.** Attorney Erica Johnstone, who represents women affected by online harassment, often makes a PSA for anyone looking for love online: confidence and romance scams—in which a con artist preys on vulnerable individuals, convincing them they have found love, and later taking advantage of them—are on the rise. She recommends we assume everyone that we meet on a dating site is a person attempting to infiltrate our business or family. Women can be sexually assaulted or have their money—sometimes even their life's savings—stolen in these situations.

Online security tips for travel

Traveling presents its own set of online safety and security precautions, particularly if you are traveling in a country where surveillance is common or women face widespread cultural, religious, or state-sponsored discrimination. If you are doing sensitive work or engaging in sensitive communications, or if you simply want to take extra precautions with your personal information and data, you might consider the following safeguards:

1. **Notify colleagues, employers, and loved ones of assignments or other travel you're undertaking alone.** Tell them when to expect you back or establish check-in times for days-long trips. Provide these allies each other's contact information to use in case of emergency and send them all your overall trip itinerary including your flight information, hotel or apartment location and contact information, as well as the micro-itineraries for any side excursions or assignments you plan to undertake.

2. **Register with your country's embassy.** Most embassies have a form to do this on their website under their consular services section. You'll fill out a form indicating your trip dates and contact information. This may seem a tempting step to avoid, but in case of a lost passport, phone, ongoing online or offline harassment in an unfriendly country, or something like the outbreak of a pandemic and closure of international borders, you'll be better off if the embassy knows you're in town.

3. We covered this in the last section, but **sharing your real-time location is especially dangerous while traveling.** Security services and petty criminals can use it to target you. It's better to wait to share those photos of sights and adventures when you're safely relaxing in your room.

4. If you deal with sensitive information or work in a sensitive industry, **bring and use a mobile burner phone.** When you land in your destination, keep your everyday, personal device disconnected from the internet and mobile networks and disable Bluetooth. Using a VPN and encrypted communications, conduct your business from your burner phone, either on a local mobile network or private WiFi. If you must, connect to public WiFi with the understanding that it puts you at increased risk. When you arrive home, perform a factory reset on the device.

5. Similarly, **consider using a cloud-based computing system during the duration of your visit.** If your laptop is seized or stolen, using a cloud-based (and, ideally, encrypted) data storage system means that the thieves or security officials will not be able to easily extract

documents from the device, as they will be stored in the cloud, not on the device's hard drive. I have worked for months at a time on a pre-owned Chromebook that cost under $200. It isn't glamorous, but it's safer than the alternative: your beautiful bespoke machine and all its data stolen, to be seen again only in the context of a disinformation operation.

6. Finally, **turn off facial and fingerprint recognition and switch to complex passwords before you cross the border.** This is another mild inconvenience that makes it a little more difficult for governments and others to easily access (what little data will be stored on) your devices.

Combined with the daily security practices you've learned in the rest of this chapter, both you and your data will be safer while traveling.

If you're learning all this information for the first time, taking charge of your online security can absolutely feel overwhelming. Luckily for all of us, there's a bit of a "set it and forget it" feel to all of these practices. Once I set up my password manager, my multi-factor authentication, and my anti-doxing subscription, they generally just run in the background while I continue my work. My other habits—moving my communications to encrypted platforms and the precautions I take to protect my physical security—take a little more daily consideration, but now that they're operationalized, they feel like part of my normal life.

If you're just getting started in protecting your digital security, make yourself a to-do list of a small change you'll make each week or month until you've fortified your online presence. For someone starting from square one, it might look something like this:

- Set up password manager
- Use password manager to reset passwords on all critical websites
- Set up two-factor authentication on all key accounts
- Talk to friends and family about moving your text conversations to encrypted platforms

- Research anti-doxing services and decide whether to sign up
- Review social media presence and consider what details a malicious individual could ascertain from posting habits; delete problematic posts and engage with care in the future.

For Cindy Otis, for me, and for the rest of the women you'll hear from in this book and many others in public life, this is the reality of our external engagement. These practices are burdens women are typically forced to shoulder without the help of their employers. Unfortunately, they are not issues that will disappear with the passage of a law or a renaissance of recommitment within social media platforms. Their root cause is the systemic misogyny we face in everyday life. Yes, taking precautions with your online security is fairly easy to do, but these practices don't come without a cost, both psychological and monetary. None of my public communication is truly spontaneous anymore. Of course, I'm willing to give up that spontaneity for my safety. Recognizing that sad fact is a reality of being a woman online.

TL;DR (for the uninitiated, internet-speak for "too long; didn't read")

1. **Use a password manager, ideally an external service that allows two-factor authentication and can generate complex passwords for you.** Avoid using single sign-on services provided by internet giants to log into sites across the internet.
2. **Set up two-factor authentication on all accounts that allow it.** Using an app or physical security key is safer than a text message code.
3. **Use an encrypted messenger and a VPN,** but remember, the recipients of your messages can still screenshot them, and message archives might be stored in the cloud unless you (and your friends) proactively turn this feature off.

4. **Consider signing up for an anti-doxing service to clean up publicly accessible information about you** sooner rather than later if you have any degree of public-facing work, especially speaking, publishing, or media commentary.

5. **Be careful about the details you share online.** Online violence can and does move offline. Don't lead the bad guys to your door by sharing photos of your location or details about the patterns in your life.

6. **Take precautions when traveling**, especially to countries with patterns of digital surveillance or if you fear offline extensions of your online harassment.

2

Adversity: Enduring Trolls

Nicole Perlroth decided to give up Twitter.

Fresh off the release of her first book, *This is How They Tell Me the World Ends*, which details the growth of the cyber arms market, the *New York Times*' cybersecurity reporter decided she had had enough. In her male-dominated field, she received a near-constant barrage of abusive content. She had finally reached her breaking point. "One thing I don't think people realize," a frustrated Nicole tweeted in late February 2021, "is how many of the same men who publicly direct vitriol female journalists' way then try to slip into their DMs with 'but really I think you're great.'"[1] She included two screenshots with her tweet. In the first, a man criticized her for posting a quote from Sacha Baron Cohen about online harassment, alleging Nicole thought herself "immune from ridicule." In the second, the same man thanked her for writing about cybersecurity in a polite and conciliatory direct message. "Twitter has become such a destructive and silencing force ... that I do not plan to be here much longer,"[2] she continued. Within days, she took a long hiatus from the platform.

The reaction was years in the making. The responses that Nicole gets to her work on cybersecurity—a very male, very insular community— are regularly laden with gendered and misogynistic tropes and insults. She frequently shares bylines with a prominent male cybersecurity journalist, David Sanger. After working together on coverage of Russia's increasing ransomware attacks in late 2020, she told him she was "exhausted from some of the reactions to our story," she recalls.[3] "David was like, 'What reaction?' He had no idea, had not seen any of it, had not gotten any of it." Meanwhile, Nicole "felt like someone had put me in a dryer and left me on high for two days." Over the years, Nicole has received everything from tweets asserting that "we're the experts and you're a little dear,"[4] to rape threats.

When Nicole's book, *This is How They Tell Me the World Ends*, was released, the abuse ballooned. She describes the book as "the history of the cyber arms market, but also my personal journey into the cyber arms market." Given that personalized frame, she prepared herself for harassment. "I knew this would happen because it was written for a lay reader," Nicole says. "That was why it took me seven years to write this book. I knew they would be hyper critical. They're myopic, and they're misogynist."

Her worries were borne out. "People who didn't even read the book were rage tweeting at me to say they would never read the book." What should have been a celebratory, positive moment in Nicole's life became stressful, saddening, and frightening. "The signal to noise ratio got so out of control. It got really gross," Nicole says. On February 26, she tweeted:

> "I joined Twitter 13 years ago. Thank you to those who brought value and humor to this platform, but it has become a destructive and silencing force for too many, especially women and minorities, and today I'm quitting. Please feel free to reach me on LinkedIn or via the NYT."[5]

Nicole recalls how difficult the decision was for her. She had tried hard over the years to engage in what she thought was a constructive way. But Twitter was no longer a constructive place for her personally or professionally. She also wanted to make the point that the cybersecurity community does itself a disservice when it harasses journalists. Nicole spent several months away from the platform, promoting her book through events, preparing for the series she would co-produce based on the book's research and reporting, and continuing to cover an increasingly important beat for *The New York Times*, as the beginning of 2021 saw an increase in ransomware attacks and cybercrime. Though her Twitter hiatus was shielding her from abuse, she realized, "wait a second. I can't do my job if I'm not on Twitter. I've silenced myself here, and I have important things to say."

She slowly made her way back onto the platform, but she notes, "I don't engage the way I used to ... I [do it] in a less authentic way. I think of [Twitter] as a way to broadcast my stories and monitor for breaking news." Nicole's experience is one frustratingly familiar to many women with public profiles. We are constantly weighing the utility of subjecting ourselves to gender-motivated abuse and harassment in exchange for fulfilling the basic duties of our jobs.

This calculation is familiar for Van Badham, an Australian activist, playwright, and columnist for *The Guardian*. Van has been subject to all manner of online—and internet-inspired offline—violence. On the day of her father's funeral, an anonymous troll sent her abusive pornography with the caption "this is what your father thought of you."[6] In 2016, she was a guest on Australia's flagship current affairs program, *Q and A*. One of Van's co-panelists, right-wing radio commentator Steve Price, told her she was being "hysterical" when she made an impassioned plea to deconstruct the cultural norms that made domestic violence common in the country—one in six Australian women is the victim of domestic abuse.[7] Speaking for women everywhere, Van responded "it's probably my ovaries making me do it, Steve," and became an instant internet meme; the hashtag #MyOvariesMadeMe trended on Australian Twitter.[8]

Women rallied around Van's empowering retort, but the misogynists of the internet seethed. "I got thousands of death threats in a couple days," Van told me. "It was really, really bad. It was every channel: Facebook, Twitter, Instagram, email. Full on sexual stuff as well." Compounding the incident, Van's life was touched by tragedy that week. "I got news that one of my closest friends died in a car accident. It was this horrendous, heartbreaking grief. It was a great lesson that the internet doesn't care about your grief. You can't put a letter up and say 'hey everyone, my friend just died, can you please stop.'"

She and her partner decided to take a vacation and internet hiatus to escape the constant barrage of abuse. Not long into the trip, recovering on the island of Phuket, Van got more devastating news. "Somebody had hacked my Twitter account and was tweeting these awful things," including Van's supposed sexual fantasies and preferences. Later, Van "found out it was a fifteen year old boy in Sweden who was doing it. Steve Price had found purchase in some internet community. It had been coordinated. I had been sacrificed 'for the lulz,'" Van recalls, using the term that troll culture coined to describe their culture of sadistic online torture for fun.

As Van climbed the ladder in three fields—activism, theater, and political commentary—the abuse challenging her, her livelihood, and her position only piled higher. She describes how people she has blocked on Twitter have become "obsessed with a persona they've created" for her, which she calls the "the folk villain version" of herself. "This version of me- I hate that person. I have a real problem for being criticized for things I did not do."

People's hatred for the fictitious version of Van has even endangered her physical safety. "There was an internet hate group dedicated to me," she says. "They were mutilating pictures of my face and making unbelievable claims about my sex life," in one breath both deriding her appearance and denying her any claim to an identity other than that of a sexual being. She has been attacked on the street and stalked, and even been forced to file a restraining order with the Australian police. She warns theaters where she works that her presence may attract unsavory characters and create security risks.

Van's conclusion from these experiences is sobering: "This is the internet. No one can protect you."

What do trolls want?

I have never met Nicole or Van in person, but I am proud to call them friends. Thanks to Twitter, I found their work and struck up a conversation. When I have been in the thick of some of the worst abuse I've experienced, they have offered their support. When they have been at the center of the online storm, I have sent them messages of solidarity.

They have both developed their own strategies for self-protection and preservation. They both recognize that the ultimate "win" for their abusers would be to turn down their online engagement, to protect their accounts, to stop writing and speaking.

Van notes: "I'm from an activist background. I've done my time. I've been beaten by police and been handcuffed and had my hair ripped out ...but it doesn't mean shit now because I have a column at *The Guardian* and more Twitter followers than most people." In today's internet culture, that notoriety—and the abuse that accompanies it—can come as a shock. "You may not think you're famous, but if other people do, you're in trouble." In her opinion, the abuse she has experienced is "about a bizarre idea that other people are more entitled to influence than you are, and if they can take you out, or make you go silent, give you a nervous breakdown, or kill yourself, then they can take that space." But in that terrifying realization is a more empowering one, Van says. "The only influence they have is over you."

Lest we think this behavior can be explained by a confluence of misogynists in their basements, feminist author and activist Soraya Chemaly writes in *Rage Becomes Her* that these campaigns are deliberate and coordinated, particularly in the realm of politics: "Graphic sexualizing of woman politicians and candidates isn't 'harmless' fun, it's a political strategy. Research shows that sexual objectification sullies a woman's reputation, degrades viewers' perceptions of the person's moral standing and competence, and demonstrably hurts her chances of being elected."[9] Nicole Perlroth notes the roots of such campaigns run deep. They're the "inevitable result of our culture, not personalizing [abuse]. Depersonalizing it. Understanding that it's not just sexist dynamics at play but cultural dynamics and community." Yes, you read right: there are entire communities of people on the internet dedicated to silencing outspoken, expert women.

Silencing us may be what trolls want, but we should not be willing to comply in order to cater to their comfort. So how do we make our way in this booby-trapped online world? Van often reminds herself that the abuse she experiences "is not a problem to be solved, it's an ongoing tension to be managed." The way we, as women of the internet and the world, manage that tension, is an intensely personal decision. No two strategies balancing engagement with safety will look the same. They will take into account support from friends, family, and employers. They will differ for women of color, trans women, and women representing other marginalized communities, who experience far greater online harm than their white counterparts. What this chapter will do—with Nicole and Van's help—is walk you through the trolls you'll encounter and the approaches you can use to manage their presence in your life.

Troll Safari

One of the most surprising phenomena I've encountered since I began making television appearances in 2017 is the sudden proliferation of men in my Twitter mentions, my email inbox, my Instagram and Facebook followers, and my direct messages. The most innocuous (but still unsettling and creepy) ones simply follow you in droves on their social media platform of choice after an appearance. I get off the air, and within minutes, my Facebook or Instagram account is flooded with notifications of man after man after man staring at me from behind their avatars after quietly clicking the follow button. On Twitter, the platform most aligned with my work, where I have tens of thousands of anonymous followers, I would think nothing of it. But the idea that these men have sought out the personal platforms where I often share images of myself, and done so immediately after seeing me on television, makes my skin crawl. I can think of a single time when a young woman followed me on Instagram after a TV appearance; she sent me a message to tell me how inspiring she found my commentary. The men, on the other hand, mostly just lurk, sometimes liking long strings of my selfies in binges of scrolling and double-tapping.

Unfortunately there are many denizens of the internet who are much more vocal than the lurkers. It is helpful to be acquainted with their various incarnations before you encounter them so you do not mistake their initial approach as anything other than bad-faith. They burst violently into your mentions and your life like the Kool-Aid man, demanding your attention, hawking opinions that they believe are unarguably, manifestly correct and indispensable. "PAY ATTENTION TO ME!" they bellow. "MY OPINION MATTERS!" What drives much of this behavior, whether it is laden with misogynistic slurs or couched in outwardly polite language, is what Van Badham calls "the engagement boner"—when users get so excited about interacting with someone whose opinion they value that they cross the line into pestering, harassing, or abusive behavior. It is a phenomenon present overwhelmingly in male users, she says, in her characteristically colorful way. "They just absolutely get the hardest goddamn dick stick of their life because you, a celebrity, are talking to them. That means—automatic proof!—that you are at least their equal or probably their inferior." It's difficult to put off men with engagement boners. If you ignore them, Van says, "they will keep trying to provoke you and continue the conversation and tagging in their friends as well ... if you block them, it's like dealing with a teenage boy who insists he has blue balls."

The engagement boner rears its ugly head in any genus of troll you encounter online. The trolls may write differently, or lash out differently, or become grotesquely fixated on different parts of your appearance or background, but ultimately, what motivates them is engagement with you. This, they hope, will encourage you to finally shut up and make room for their infinitely more worthy thoughts. They will get the blue check, the TV appearances, the bylines. They will curse and block and post hot takes with alacrity and abandon. And in their mind, the internet will praise them for it. Their motivations are undoubtedly repulsive, but I find that humor is a good antidote to troll-induced repulsion. Let's meet some of these creatures.

- **@ProfessorActuallyEsq: the reply guy.** Every woman with a public presence online has at least one reply guy. Most women have several. If you are especially unlucky, or especially prominent, you might have tens or hundreds. (Groan!) @ProfessorActuallyEsq embodies them. He is a man who responds to what feels like every single earthly thing you post, be it a picture of your breakfast or your latest publication, always unearthing the most tenuous connection to make your content, your life, about him. "Actually, next time leave the toast in a little longer," he lectures you about your bacon, egg, and cheese. "It should be golden brown." You may have liked a reply of his, once, eons ago, encouraging his engagement boner. He is often a mansplainer, making sure to assert his pseudo-superiority by explaining the topics in which you have expertise. Sometimes he repeats your own points back to you, or better still, links you to the very articles you wrote in arguments with you. If you share a fresh piece you wrote about the national security threat that systemic misogyny poses, as I did, he will reply, "Actually, China, Russia, and Iran use misogynistic tropes in their disinformation campaigns." Thank you, oh wise one, @ProfessorActuallyEsq, for opening my eyes to the horrors of being a woman online. I could have *never* made the argument about which I just wrote and published 1500 words without *you*! Sometimes these men are credentialed, and like @ProfessorActuallyEsq, they are not afraid to remind you of that. Professors of philosophy, law, and engineering; former high-ranking diplomats; and current businessmen, all engage in behavior that we can only hope does not show up in their classrooms or offices. (Except it definitely does.)

- **@TrojanHorace: the bait and switch guy.** As a writer and commentator, I get a lot of engagement, leads, and opportunities through my direct messages on social media. Leaving my DMs open is a necessity for my work, though it does sometimes expose me to dick pics, romantic propositions, and other unwanted attention and abuse. Sometimes I receive positive messages expressing solidarity with me when I post about online harassment, thanking me for my work, or congratulating me on a recent publication. I thought these messages were a lovely antidote to the vitriol and sexism on the rest of the internet, until I encountered @TrojanHorace. His initial approach is one of allyship or admiration. When you reply with an off-the-cuff, "Thanks, I appreciate it!" @TrojanHorace understands this to mean that you are now equals or friends. Engagement boner activated. One thing he knows for sure: you are interested in having a longer conversation with him. Here, his tactics shift. He may err toward the behavior of his pal, @ProfessorActuallyEsq, offering to educate you. He may ask you unsettling questions about what you're wearing or what you had for dinner. He may send you voice memos that you are too afraid to open because of what unspeakable sounds they might contain. If you attempt to gracefully bow out of the conversation after it takes this upsetting turn, @TrojanHorace becomes hostile, employing the same misogyny at which he was so recently aghast. Because of @TrojanHorace, I no longer answer kind messages from strangers. This is why we can't have nice things.

- **@LazyLogan: the man who can't seem to use Google.** There are a lot of lazy people—mostly men—who seem to think women's purpose on the internet is not to inform others about their expertise, analyze the news, or amplify their work, but to answer inane questions about basic concepts about which they could easily educate themselves. Instead, they seem to prefer to ask you to do it. While researching and writing this book and tweeting my related thoughts and updates, I've received questions like: What is SWATing? What is an anti-doxing service? These easily-googled queries are a double-whammy of subversion; if you answer, @LazyLogan's engagement boner is rewarded, and you prove yourself to be a compliant and dutiful human encyclopedia. If only the men like @LazyLogan were aware how needy, infantile, and incapable they made themselves look in the process.

- **DwightDooley1936@hotmail.com: THE OLD MAN WHO EMAILS YOU IN ALL CAPS.** HE IS NOT ON SOCIAL MEDIA SO HE TOOK THE TIME TO LOOK UP YOUR ELECTRONIC MAIL ADDRESS AFTER SEEING YOU ON THE TV. HE DISAGREES WITH WHAT YOU SAY, THOUGH HE DOESN'T

SEEM SURE IF HE DISAGREES WITH THE SUBSTANCE OR
THE FACT THAT IT IS COMING OUT OF YOUR FEMININE
PIE HOLE PAINTED WITH TARTY RED LIPSTICK!!!! ONE
THING IS CLEAR: YOU, MISSY, ARE TOO BIG FOR YOUR
BRITCHES—OR I SUPPOSE WE SHOULD SAY "MINISKIRT!"
HA HA HA! IF YOU MAKE THE MISTAKE OF RESPONDING
TO DWIGHT WITH A PROFESSIONAL COLD SHOULDER
("Thank you for reaching out, but my research indicates otherwise
…), HOPING THIS WILL MAKE HIM GO AWAY, HE WILL
DOUBLE DOWN AND CALL YOU UPPITY. ALL OF HIS
EMAILS ARE NO FEWER THAN FIVE PARAGRAPHS LONG
AND INCLUDE HIS LOCATION, AS IF IN SUBMISSION TO
THE EDITORIAL BOARD OF YOUR BRAIN.

- **@AntiFeministFrank: the men's rights activists, incels, neo-Nazis, and proto-fascists.** I have a folder full of abuse I've received
from the scum of the internet: the man who shouts about the
scourge of feminism and believes that women who work, think,
and speak up are upsetting the natural balance of the universe. Our
main occupation, he asserts, should be to birth babies, care for
them, and get dinner on the table for our manly husbands every
day from nine months after our first menstrual cycle to the
beginning of menopause. @AntiFeministFrank (who, by the way,
loves to share images of "traditional" women in the post-Second
World War era in A-line dresses, crinoline petticoats, and kitten
heels, and wants to return to a world of cheery Sally Homemakers
who quietly abused alcohol and tranquilizers) cannot let an
opportunity to ridicule a woman's appearance or sexuality pass. He
will point out a woman's wrinkles ("I bet you were pretty when you
were younger, like my 26-year-old woman is now"), send her
pictures of empty egg cartons (a reminder of her decreasing
fertility), or make more explicitly sexual comments ("No wonder
you're a single mom. Did your ex-husband have to wear a blindfold
when he impregnated you?"). He may be a member of the
involuntary celibate ("incel") community, believes feminism is the

scourge of the century, and will often subscribe to far-right-leaning political beliefs, including fascist ideologies. Sadly, these tendencies do show themselves across the political spectrum, particularly when men feel themselves challenged by younger, more capable women who would never spare a thought for engaging with them, intellectually or romantically.

A note on fake or seedy accounts. Have you ever gotten friend or follow requests on closed platforms like Facebook, Instagram, or LinkedIn from people you don't know and aren't sure actually exist? It's important to be extra wary of these accounts as some of them might be attempting to add you in order to collect your personal information for the nefarious purposes discussed in the previous chapter. You should ask yourself the following questions when evaluating one of these requests:

- When was the account created? If it was recently but somehow the account still boasts a lot of followers or content, it may be fake.
- Does it have a profile picture? Is it unique or generic? Does a reverse image search lead you to conclude the profile picture is stolen from another person? Accounts without profile pictures, with generic photos, or with stolen photos may be inauthentic.
- Do you have any friends or followers in common? If a random person from a far-flung locale is messaging you out of the blue, ignore.
- Generally, if anything about the account seems off, trust your gut and deny the friend request. If this person really wants to get in touch for benign reasons, they will reach out and make themselves known.

Dealing with Trolls

The prevailing advice that every woman in the throes of online abuse has received is "just ignore it." "Don't feed the trolls," we are told, while the alleged asymmetry of our faces is publicly discussed, our every wrinkle and pimple amplified, our breast size or weight ridiculed, and the most beautiful, self-affirming images of ourselves on the internet contorted and edited to hideous caricatures meant to demonstrate how unfit we are for human interaction, let alone influence. I have been told I am a living argument for the repeal of the Nineteenth Amendment, which gave voting rights to women. I embody the utility of Sharia Law, my trolls say. This is the type of behavior in which men are granted free license to engage, while we are supposed to sit idly by and endure it, smiling. Better yet, we are told to "be the bigger person" and find empathy for our trolls, who must have difficult lives if they are acting out in this way. Responding in anger will only make things worse, we are reminded. Women are expected to stoically endure astronomical levels of abuse to simply participate in conversations while navigating a set of social mores and boundaries that simply don't exist for men. When men encounter behavior they don't like online, they curse. They block. They willingly and openly dogpile and troll. And the world thinks them more manly for it. Women, in calling out much worse behavior, are told we are "emotional," "weak," "exaggerating," or—as Van Badham was described—"hysterical."

"Being closemouthed is a feminine quality," Soraya Chemaly writes. "Women are especially not supposed to question or publicly shame men for their behavior. If they use their public voices to address topics that go beyond gender roles, families, and appearance—particularly if they challenge that limitation—they can count on public hostility, off- and online."[10]

Van Badham agrees. In a *Guardian* essay called "Twitter, the barbarian country, or how I learned to love the block button," she notes that "Girls are socialized 'from an early age not to promote their own interests and to focus instead on the needs of others,' even when those others are baying hordes of anonymous mansplainers, desperate—just desperate—to yell at a void the same gender as their mum."[11] It is these social mores—the way girls are brought up from infancy, the feminine characteristics of care and kindness that are praised when we are coworkers in office environments—that make us hesitant to take charge of the online environment in which we not only exist, but play a vital role. Laura Bates, the founder of the Everyday Sexism Project, told Chemaly, "we are so socialized to accept this treatment that we don't realize we have the right to anger in the moment."[12] That anger, Chemaly argues, is a valuable resource. The "social costs of pointing out prejudice are high," she affirms, "but when women recognize discrimination and the anger it provokes, this heightened consciousness yields positive effects, such as the ability to strategize and confront problems."[13]

Perhaps you *will* choose to simply ignore the next troll that appears in your replies. But there are moments when and approaches with which calling out bad behavior is not only necessary; it can be *healthy* to make your voice heard, both for you and your fellow women online. There are ways to manage trolls' tantrums while still protecting your brand, your psyche, and yourself.

So how should we approach @ProfActuallyEsq? Does dealing with him require a different response than @TrojanHorace or @AntiFeministFrank? That is entirely up to you, but this is the arsenal you have at the ready.

For your own mental health, **mute and move on.** Once you identify the annoying mosquito men of the internet, like @ProfActuallyEsq and @LazyLogan, it is tempting to swat them away with a sarcastic reply. You are a queen who has limited time and resources to spend on these men; they are not worth the energy. The most economical response is to mute (or unfollow) and move on. We will discuss the structural advantages of embracing these affordances of platform infrastructure in the next chapter, but until then, enjoy the image of these swarms simply buzzing around in a vacuum, shouting into a void, where there are no potential hosts for their parasitic behavior. The best part of this approach is they'll never know they've been muted. Bliss.

Embrace blocktivism. Similarly, when someone gets truly nasty, he (or she) does not deserve the charity of the mute button. They deserve to be in social media jail. We must, Van Badham says, "embrace blocktivism."

Your social media profiles are a queendom, not a democracy, she reminds me, and (unless you are an American elected official, in which case the legality of blocking constituents is a bit thorny) you have the right to make the rules and block early and often. "Beyond blocking outright Nazis and haters, I've now permitted myself to block the petty, the hostile, nasty, monomaniacal ... even the merely tiresome," Van wrote in her *Guardian* essay:

> *Ten thousand accounts I've banished from my feed to render the medium*
> *as exciting as I once imagined that it could be. Affirmed here is not only*
> *my right to select my own company, but also to return to the standards I*
> *once applied to reading newspapers; I've got time to digest the op-eds*
> *because I've skipped the chess puzzles and car section.*[14]

Nicole Perlroth also found blocking to be a necessity for her reengagement with social media. She uses a woman-developed tool called BlockParty to assist in her efforts. For a small fee, this app combs through your Twitter mentions and identifies and filters out accounts that might be abusive. You can then log onto the service and check your "Lockout" folders, where you can block individuals based on their behavior. Nicole found this segmentation extremely useful. "I put on the strictest controls, and I would look at the Lockout folders, and I would start blocking anyone who was being rude," she says. "Of course, I got a lot of backlash for being 'too sensitive,' but it did help a lot." At this writing, BlockParty only interfaces only with Twitter, though CEO Tracy Chou has plans to expand it to other social media platforms.[15] BlockParty also allows you to designate a "helper" who can sift through your Lockout folder so you can insulate yourself from an ongoing wave of abuse.

There are downsides to blocking, or, even more extreme, temporarily locking down your account. Cindy Otis, the former CIA analyst we met in the last chapter, never engages with trolls. "The whole point of trolling is to get others to help them elevate their message," she notes. By blocking and going on "lockdown, you are absolutely giving [trolls] what they are hoping to achieve." But, she says, it's not something that bothers her. "For me, personal safety is my biggest concern when it comes to trolling. I would encourage people to put their personal safety first."

In the next chapter, we'll discuss how blocking sends important signals to social media platforms' algorithms, helping them detect future abuse. For now, remember that the block button is meant to protect you and restore some sanctity to your social media experience. You don't need to explain your reasons for using it.

Don't bomb the village. There will be a time when you choose to reply to something abusive that is sent to you. In the moment, it may feel like the most logical, fair, and effective response is to name and shame the anonymous @FartEater account arguing with you or harassing you. But the internet is not logical or fair, and this response may lead to reputational damage and further trolling. "Don't take the bait," says Van Badham. "That's what they want." Particularly when you are engaging with a low-follower, low-notoriety account that is not operating in good faith, you may score a sick burn, but you are also amplifying this person and giving them precious online oxygen.

There may be times you are inundated by many @FartEaters. Picking them off, one by one, with devastating one-liners, is appealing, but inadvisable. "There's a psychological payoff to swatting a fly," Van notes, "but to the outside, it looks like you're bombing a village ... Bombing a village is a successful short-term strategy, but long-term, it is as successful as bombing a village has ever been ... it becomes a branding problem." Here, it is helpful to recall the tragic storyline of Daenerys Targaryen, the dragon-riding queen in the *Game of Thrones* series. (Spoilers ahead.) Daenerys decides to sack the capital city after enduring years of exile, obstacles, and adversity. Ultimately, this decision leads to her downfall. Don't be Daenerys.

However, I do *completely* understand the desire to raise awareness about bad behavior and the prevalence of abuse and harassment for women in public life. There is nothing more frustrating than sitting idly by, seething, while your trolls continue their self-interested rampage around the internet. That's why I've adopted the following approach that allows me to call out abusers, put a spotlight on their tactics, and maintain my voice and agency, rather than be bullied into silence.

Deny influence and notoriety. Here's how I do it. I take a screenshot of the offending tweet, comment, post, or email. I erase all evidence of the sender's existence. Their profile picture of a woman in a bikini or a racist Pepe the Frog? Gone. Idiotic display name including their height and IQ? Obliterated. Handle inevitably containing an offensive slur? Redacted. All that's left is their sad, insecure, needy words, which I then pick apart and share. My followers often demand I unmask these trolls; I refuse. If they like, they can locate the offending content with a little effort, but most people choose not to expend it. In one fell swoop, I've denied my abusers the influence and notoriety (and engagement boner) they crave. I have pointed out how unacceptable their behavior is, and I have stopped the cycle of counter-vitriol that often explodes online. I don't always follow my own advice—sometimes the desire to dunk gets the better of me (I am only human, after all)—but when I do, I notice that my trolls seem to give up and move on. I like to think I perhaps drove them to a bout of introspection; a girl's got to dream.

The screenshot approach also works well if a high-profile individual is behaving reprehensibly, but engaging directly (with a quote tweet or reply on Twitter, or a tag or comment on Facebook) will risk opening up a new onslaught of abuse. Unless someone "snitch tags" the account in question, antagonistically tagging their profile to alert them of your animosity (or attempting to support you by tagging the account in rage, not realizing there was a reason you did not do so), you can raise awareness of their bad behavior without sharing your online oxygen tank with them.

Laugh at them. A key component of my own self-preservation—a category distinct, but just as important as preserving your safety and online brand—has been humor. Without the ability to laugh at and poke fun at my abusers along with other women who know exactly what I'm going through (almost always in private, so as not to invite more harassment), I would be frightened and despondent. It can be all but impossible to find that humor in the moment you are at the center of an online swarm. But there is nothing juicier than having a laugh at @AntiFeministFrank's expense, and later relegating him to shout into the endless, echoing void as you smash the block button.

Nicole is back on Twitter, albeit in a limited way. She's determined to continue to report on the critical topics of her cybersecurity beat, but is frustrated with the lack of action for women experiencing online harassment and how impotent she feels in response. "I don't think people understand the viciousness of it, and how much of it women get, and that it just doesn't end. And there's no clear way to respond to it, except silence, muting the accounts, blocking the accounts." Even understanding that, Nicole notes that the abuse she has experienced "does have a silencing effect, for sure, even for someone who's a reporter at *The New York Times*."

Van continues to endure gendered internet invectives, walking even farther into the digital fire as she works on a new book about the QAnon conspiracy theory. She recently deactivated her Facebook account, where she had long maintained both professional and "friends-only" pages. After another trolling campaign against her in autumn 2021, she understood that as a woman with a public profile "your intimacy becomes a commodity that can be transacted. Old friends betrayed me because [on Facebook] your personal musings are screen-cappable and shareable." But closing her Facebook account has made it easier to flip the switch between her public and private selves. "After I deleted Facebook, I've been a lot happier. I don't feel the complex social weight of that intimate persona. If I want to bring someone into an intimate community, I've got to do it in person." Deleting Facebook has also led Van to a new level of caution on her

Twitter account, she says. "I don't give as much personal information as I used to. [Your followers are] not your friends, They're not all following you because they like you."

Since my own trolling experience in the lead-up to the 2020 U.S. presidential election, I have gotten a lot less patient and a lot more mute-and-block-happy. My first reaction to a random stranger online is no longer one of tolerance; before all else, it is distrust. At times that upsets me, and I pour one out for the internet I and other women deserve, but cannot access. Just as Van despises the folk villain version of herself that the internet has created, I know that the dumb, disfigured, CIA operative, deep state bimbo the internet claims I am has no basis in reality. I am none of those things, and more importantly, I am not a bad person. I ended up in my line of work—researching disinformation and abuse—because of my intense desire to help people, to make change, and yet I've been lambasted not only for that choice, but because of an innate characteristic: my gender. The tradeoffs we face as women online are infuriating. That's why it is so critical we call out this behavior—and the infrastructure that enables it—in a way that builds awareness while preserving our safety and sanity.

TL;DR

1. **Trolls range from the merely annoying to the appalling and grotesque.** Some behavior merits a response. Lots of it merits a simple mute or a block. Don't bomb the village.
2. **Trolls want your attention.** They benefit from your engagement with them; don't take the bait.
3. **Trolls want to silence you.** They do this because they believe they can gain your influence (of which they feel they are infinitely more worthy) once you fade away. Don't let them.
4. **Women are socialized to be accommodating, but your social media profiles are not a democracy.** Use the tools at your disposal

however you wish to use them. You don't owe anyone an explanation for protecting yourself.

5. **This is a problem to be managed, not solved.** Unfortunately, trolls will never go away. We cannot control them, but we *can* control how we react.

3

Policy: Making it Work for You

In 2014, Brianna Wu was forced to flee her home. She paused her successful career as a video game developer when she became the subject of a relentless stream of online abuse and death threats. The online and offline violence against her and two other women in the gaming industry was so horrific it inspired an episode of the popular police procedural *Law & Order*. But Brianna did not back down: "I'm doing everything I can to save my life except be silent," she wrote five months after the explosion of online abuse known as "Gamergate" trained its menace on her.[1]

For the uninitiated, Gamergate was a months-long coordinated harassment campaign against women in the video game industry, from game development to media. Brianna was one of its targets. Using the hashtag #Gamergate, Brianna's abusers presented her, Zoë Quinn, and Anita Sarkeesian—the women at the center of the campaign—with what they viewed as a simple choice: the women could stop making critiques of the misogyny of the gaming industry, or they would face abuse and encouragement to leave their careers. Despite credible threats to her life, Brianna continued to speak up. For nearly a decade, she has been a tireless advocate for other women enduring similar online abuse.

Gamergate was a high-profile and shocking explosion of misogynistic abuse that *The New York Times*' Charlie Warzel believes "changed the way we fight online."[2] But systematic sexism, discrimination, and harassment of women online—particularly women of color and other marginalized identities—was nothing new for the tech industry. A year before Gamergate exploded, Adria Richards, a Black software developer, tweeted about sexism in the tech industry. She shamed two male attendees at a developer's conference for joking about "big dongles"—a tired double entendre referring to USB drives (known as dongles) and male sex organs—while they attended a panel about encouraging gender diversity in tech. As a result of her tweet, Richards was targeted with sexist abuse herself. Later, she was fired; her employer wrote that Richards' "decision to tweet the comments and photographs of people who made the comments crossed the line."[3] This wasn't an isolated incident; at the same time as Donglegate, fringe groups from anonymous discussion boards were increasingly impersonating and targeting Black feminists online, attempting to sully their reputations and drive them out of public discourse.

The next year, Gamergate made headlines as women in the video game industry were also faced with relentless harassment and violent threats. Brianna Wu watched the abuse and threats mount and grew angrier. Online abusers "were bullying my friends out of the industry one by one," she recalls. "I saw men in the industry that were not doing anything about it. I had brutal arguments with a lot of [them], asking them to stand up for their women colleagues. I went to war the best I could because I saw no help was coming from the men in our field."[4] She spoke out. She was threatened. She filed police reports. She met with tech companies. She worked with the FBI and the Obama White House. And nothing changed. "I wish I could tell you that it's gotten better," Brianna wrote in *The New York Times* in 2019. "It hasn't. Gamergate gave birth to a new kind of celebrity troll, men who made money and built their careers by destroying women's reputations."[5] That destruction touched her loved ones. In our conversation, she recalls how "a friend made the specific decision to get out of the public eye because she was afraid her children were going to get killed."

It was the devastating decisions like this that led Brianna to her advocacy. Brianna also ran for Congress, announcing her candidacy not long after the 2016 election ushered in the Trump era.[6] "What I think is so sad about my experience in 2014 is that it is such a common experience these days, because law enforcement made the choice to not prosecute these people," she tells me. That failure "made the Donald Trump playbook possible," Brianna asserts. Had her Congressional bid been successful, she hoped to bring her personal experience to bear while serving on the House of Representatives Committee on Science, Space, and Technology. Instead, she spun up a political action committee and continues to advocate for the voices of marginalized communities and privacy rights online.

In the years since Gamergate changed her life, Brianna has learned how to deal with trolls and abusers better than most of us will hopefully ever need to. The most important thing she's learned? "The best way to beat them is to play by the platforms' rules." It's time to discuss all the tools available to you on the most popular social media platforms, how using them makes other women's online experiences safer and more pleasant, and how to gather evidence in case you decide to take your case outside of the social media system.

Get your muting, blocking, and reporting fingers ready. We're going to neutralize some trolls.

Before we get into the nitty gritty details of social media policy, it's important to understand that navigating it really can help you. Employing a knowledge of social media platforms' terms and tools was critical when Leta Hong Fincher, an American journalist and scholar who is an expert on feminism in contemporary China, was bombarded with sexualized harassment after criticizing forced marriages in Xinjiang in summer 2020. She says she felt like "a tsunami was raging on top" of her.[7] "There were people calling me a multitude of sexualized insults, misogynistic insults ... there have been people threatening to gang rape me and rape me and referring to my children," she recalls.[8] Leta's abusers created multiple fake profiles impersonating her. Her trolls took to other platforms, too, including Leta's Amazon page, where they left inauthentic reviews of her books. Typically, Leta would block abusive accounts like these without a second thought, but in this instance, "there were so many different accounts attacking me at the same time and I just couldn't get on top of it." She wondered aloud on Twitter, "Is it any wonder that most women prefer not to call out harassers publicly?"[9]

She does credit Twitter with *some* response; as I'll detail later, after an email exchange with a Twitter employee and a public awareness campaign led by the Coalition for Women in Journalism, the platform began taking action against some of the abuse and verified Leta's account to guard against further impostors. But women without the profile, resources, or volition to escalate evidence of abuse may not have been able to achieve this result. "I know that Twitter responded to my complaints very quickly compared to a lot of other people, and I think that probably had to do with the people that I know. I got a personal introduction to the correct person at Twitter to handle that complaint, which most people wouldn't have," Leta says.

Whenever I see content on any platform that might violate the terms of service, I report it. Generally, these reports disappear into the ether; when the platforms *do* follow up with me, it is usually to tell me something to the effect of "we're sorry, but we found no violation of terms" in the rape threat you received. (Apparently, they do not believe "I'm going to rape you with a bag over your head" is targeted harassment.) Members of focus groups I have conducted have reported similarly frustrating experiences. So, when I reviewed Twitter replies to Leta from the period of the campaign against her, I was shocked at how many pieces of content had been removed and how many accounts were suspended or terminated entirely. This speaks to Brianna Wu's key advice: "read through the terms of service of the platform you're being harassed on," she tells me. On Twitter, for example, which has explicit policies against targeted harassment of trans people and deadnaming— when a trans person's previous name is used—reporting such content should get it removed immediately. "Read through those terms of service and understand when you've got them dead to rights," says Brianna.

Unfortunately, very few women have the time, resources, or wherewithal to constantly report content on social media. It is a privilege to protect oneself. Leta said the process was "exhausting" for her. Sociologist Sarah Sobieraj, who documented the impact of online misogyny on its targets in *Credible Threat*, writes in her book:

Hours and days are lost weeding through comments, Tweets, and messages. Many women invested time documenting the abuse. They organized screen shots, printed and filed materials, and otherwise worked to create a paper trail at the request of law enforcement or employers—or simply to have evidence on hand in the event of escalation. Going to court, filing reports, blocking and reporting—all these strategies sap time.[10]

Understanding policy and using it to your advantage can be cumbersome, time consuming, and extremely frustrating, but for those who have the resources and energy to do so, it is part of being a good digital citizen and protecting yourself. As of this writing, pressure on social media platforms to respond to gendered and sexualized harassment, as well as online abuse and disinformation more generally, is growing. In July 2021, Facebook, Twitter, TikTok, and Google committed to protect women on their platforms.[11] Beyond attention to this specific policy area, platforms' terms of service change frequently. In this section, I will walk you through the most important extant features to improve your online experience on key platforms. But a word of caution: it's important that you stay up to date with them. (To help you do so, there is a link to a helpful chart laying out key policy measures and platform features in the resources section at the back of this book.) They may change—or, we hope, improve!—in the future.

Muting, Blocking, and Reporting

As we learned from Van Badham in Chapter 2, your timeline is a queendom, not a democracy. You should embrace blocktivism to make the online environment a more pleasant place. On Twitter, you also have the option to mute people. This is a wonderful feature for reply guys and other less aggressive individuals, as they will never know you've muted them but you will never have to see their content again, unless you choose to. The worst of the worst, however, deserve to be blocked, not only to save your sanity, but to send an important signal to platforms. These abusers may be upset about losing their valuable access to contact with you. In some cases, blocking can spur more harassment if the banished troll shares that he has been blocked and encourages his followers to pick up his slack. They can be blocked too.

Those consequences are worth risking and enduring, because this is about more than simply making your social media experience more bearable. It also sends the platforms valuable signals about who is a serial abuser and whose account deserves a look-see from their content moderation teams. As Brianna says, "if you've got 14 followers and you're constantly getting blocked by people you interact with, that's a signal [to the platforms] that the account probably doesn't have good intentions." It will also affect the filters on incoming abuse you see on some platforms. On Twitter, when I started to mute and block more liberally, the tenor of my replies changed; the platform was no longer showing me "low-quality" replies based on my muting and blocking behavior, including content with curse words or from accounts with very few followers. You can block accounts manually, or, as discussed in the last chapter, use a tool like BlockParty to assist you in your troll-banishment crusade.

Facebook does not offer the granularity of muting in its tools; if an offending account is not in your "friends" list, your only choices are to block or report the offending content or their account. (Facebook *does* have an "unfollow" feature which allows you to stop seeing someone's posts, but remain friends. However, I sincerely hope if a "friend" is abusing you that you remove them from your friends list without a second thought.) Similarly, TikTok allows you to block and report, but not mute, individual accounts. YouTube allows users to report offending accounts, hide them from your channel, and remove individual comments. Instagram, however, allows you to "restrict" an account—making it so an abusive account's comments are only visible to the abuser—in addition to typical blocking and reporting functions.

Reporting specific content is where your familiarity with each platform's terms of service, community standards, guidelines, and rules is crucially important. During the reporting process, the platform will prompt you to choose an issue or policy area—such as targeted harassment— under which the content or account you are reporting falls. Some platforms allow you to describe the situation and add context to the content being reported; TikTok allows you to upload relevant screenshots. But no amount of supporting documentation will create consequences for abusers or relief for you if the offending content is submitted into the wrong vertical and routed to the wrong moderator. As I mentioned earlier, the resources section at the back of this book references a document outlining each platform's policy; use it to learn how platforms define the behaviors you are reporting. This understanding can also be deployed in building public support and awareness campaigns, interacting with platform representatives, and publicly holding platforms to account, as we'll discuss in the next section.

Other features to make social media less awful

Whether you're in the middle of a trolling campaign or simply don't want to deal with reply guys for another minute, you should explore and take advantage of the on-platform features that control who has access to your precious mental and emotional energy.

Twitter

Twitter has a variety of helpful tools to protect your safety and sanity. Under privacy and safety settings, for example, you can decide: who can tag you in photos, who can direct message you, and if those who have your personal information such as a phone number can find you on Twitter (helpful if you are trying to stay anonymous). You can also mute certain keywords and see the accounts you've muted and blocked. Perhaps the most important tweak is the ability to control when Twitter sends you a notification. You can pause notifications from people who don't follow you, who have a new account, who have a default profile picture, or who haven't confirmed their phone number and email. These features weed out many individuals engaging in bad faith from behind burner accounts. They can still post filth, but you won't be notified every time they do. Similarly, you can choose to turn on a "quality filter" that will, according to Twitter, "filter out duplicate or automated tweets."[12] Finally, when writing and sending tweets, you can decide who can reply to your content: everyone, people you follow, or people you've mentioned. If replies to your tweets are offensive, aggressive, or otherwise annoying (remember, your timeline is your kingdom!) you can choose to "hide" them and the content will be sent to the bottom of the replies with a click-through overlay stating "this reply was hidden by the original tweet author."[13]

Additionally, Twitter began testing "Safety Mode" in September 2021. When turned on, the feature "temporarily blocks accounts for seven days for using potentially harmful language — such as insults or hateful remarks — or sending repetitive and uninvited replies or mentions."[14] While this feature does not punish abusers, it does make weathering a storm of abuse a bit easier.

Facebook

Facebook's privacy settings, while detailed, are quite overwhelming to navigate. The company created a "privacy checkup" feature that walks you through who can see what you share, how to keep your account secure, how people can find you on the platform, your data settings, and your ad preferences.[15] One useful tool among the many that Facebook offers is the option to "limit past posts." If you're in the middle of a harassment campaign and trolls begin to attack past public posts on your profile, you can turn on this feature to change all your public or "friends of friends" posts to "friends only." The same settings menu gives users the ability to control who can send them messages and where messages from certain groups get routed—either to a main messages folder, or to a "message requests" folder. Under the "profile and tagging" menu, Facebook allows you to control who can tag you in content and mute certain keywords. The "location" menu is where you can turn off your location history on mobile devices (which I recommend you do, not only to keep yourself safe, but also to ensure the online advertising microtargeted at you is a little less creepy). Journalists can sign up to benefit from "journalist resources," which include stronger security measures like "special protection from harassment and hacking."[16] Official campaign and politician pages are also eligible for similar protections.

Instagram and TikTok

Instagram allows users detailed control over who can see and interact with their content, as well as the notifications they receive. Under privacy settings, the platform allows you to decide who can comment on your photos—everyone, people you follow, people who follow you, or both—as well as block comments from certain individuals. You can also choose to hide offensive comments and turn on a manual filter that will hide comments containing words or phrases of your choosing. Instagram gives you control over who can mention and tag you in posts and whether you manually approve those tags, and it also allows you to hide view counts on your content if you are getting a little too obsessed with "doing it for the 'gram," or, more morosely, if you're in the middle of a harassment campaign and don't want to know how many creeps have been looking at your content. As on Twitter, Instagram allows you to mute notifications from people you don't follow. As mentioned earlier, Instagram also has the helpful "restrict" feature, which limits your interactions with an account, pushing their messages to you into a requests folder, hiding your online status and read receipts from them, and requiring approval for public comments on your posts. Instagram also introduced a "harmful words" feature, allowing users to mute certain words as well as hide comments and message requests.

TikTok offers many of the same features as Instagram, also nestled under the privacy settings menu. Additionally, you can control: who can natively download your videos and create duets or stitches with them (though this won't stop people from screen recording your content with third-party apps); who can comment on your videos; and who can see what accounts you follow and the videos you've liked.

YouTube

YouTube's controls are not quite as robust as other platforms. Creators can choose to keep their videos private or unlisted as well as turn off comments on their content. The platform does offer some granular control over who can comment on a video and the words they use; creators can remove comments and their replies, flag content to YouTube, or hold potentially inappropriate comments for review. Unfortunately, more so than on other platforms, YouTube users are shouldered with most of the burden of protecting themselves and making the platform a pleasant place to engage in public discourse.

Gmail and Other Email Services

In the days after the January 6 insurrection at the U.S. Capitol, I was quoted in the *LA Times* and later received an aggressive message to my work email from a Gmail address. Among other insults, a man who evoked violence in his email address told me "you seem to be hankering for a civil war, and you might get your wish. Good fukkking [sic] luck with that." I was alarmed, especially when I found out that this man had harassed other analysts, academics, and journalists appearing in the *LA Times*. As a good citizen of the internet, I wanted to report the content to Gmail. At the time, there was no option other than to report the message as spam. Since then, Google has updated its policies to include harassment.[17] The phenomenon of strangers writing you harassing emails is unfortunately a part of many women's jobs, but when these emails are threatening or violent, we don't need to make it easy for them. Whether from Gmail or other email providers, do attempt to report accounts engaging in this behavior. It's a bit like playing Whacka-Troll, but may lead to these accounts and individuals being barred from services. Otherwise, to protect yourself from unwanted mail, you can create filters to send messages with certain keywords, from specific senders, or from those outside of your organization or contacts to another folder or straight to the trash. If you work at a well-resourced organization that can afford to dedicate a staffer to sort through your email and flag or delete abusive messages, this is another way to manage the problem. Unfortunately, most of us—especially freelancers—do not have access to such luxuries.

Another tip (tangential to platform policy but crucial to sanity) that I wish I had learned as I dove into my freelance career: if you are self-employed, separate your work email from your personal email! It may seem like an unnecessary and cumbersome step when your contacts are already stored in your personal email, but it will make putting up a wall between work and home much easier, as well as insulate you from work-related abuse after hours and on the weekends (assuming you turn off your notifications at those times).

Public Support and Solidarity Campaigns

Though Brianna and Leta's experiences with online misogyny took place seven years apart and within vastly different communities, both women made the calculation that building public support and solidarity about the campaigns against them was necessary. They understood not only that it would likely open them up to further abuse—it did, because this is the internet we're talking about—but that it could improve the situation for the women who would be targeted in the future.

Brianna immediately began tweeting, speaking, and writing about her experiences. She was profiled in *The Guardian* and *The Washington Post*, interviewed on the PBS *Newshour*, and highlighted in many tech industry publications, to list only a fraction of the media Brianna engaged with in the days after she was driven from her home. On

Newshour, she appeared exhausted as she told the interviewer "it's literally been the worst thing I've ever experienced in my life … the idea is to terrorize women in the game industry."[18] Her impassioned demand for change in her field likely reached an audience that may have otherwise never heard of Gamergate or recognized the sexism in the industry or against women online. Brianna also engaged in some behaviors she regrets: "I'm not proud of everything I did during Gamergate," she tells me, "but looking back at it I can say I tried everything." At the time, she engaged antagonistically with some of her abusers, but she no longer recommends such behavior. "One of the things I don't believe in is to harass them right back or send your followers at them. I've personally come to the conclusion that this is not ethical to do." Her new approach is about protecting her personal safety and setting the record straight at the most effective time, she says. "What I do is block mercilessly. I pick one moment … and I pick [content] that has a lot of replies, [and] put the truth out there where people can see it … Most people understand harassment and will see it and give you the benefit of the doubt."

Leta Hong Fincher took a slightly different approach. In addition to blocking and reporting content herself, she called out the misogynistic attacks on her Twitter timeline, enlisting the support of her followers to do the same. The Twitter campaign led to the publication of a letter of support from the Coalition for Women in Journalism. "Women journalists will not be intimidated and silenced by organized efforts of trolls. We acknowledge the need for criticism for the betterment of societies," the Coalition wrote.[19] All of this action culminated in Twitter's own removal of many of the attacks and the verification of Leta's account. Her campaign did not come without some repercussions; in replies to tweets from the Coalition and Leta's own account, users continued to attack Leta, though the relentlessly misogynistic attacks stopped. The trolling and doxing discussion board Kiwi Farms—a site that has perpetrated harassment campaigns connected to several suicides—started a thread on Leta that criticized her appearance as well as her ethnic and family background. It's a reminder that while much of the focus on online harassment is directed toward mainstream social media platforms, the worst abuse is perpetuated in the dark corners of the internet, ungoverned by even the lackluster terms of service that reign over large platforms like Facebook and Twitter.

If you do decide to speak out, despite the potential pitfalls of inspiring an aftershock of abuse, public support and solidarity campaigns can be incredibly useful, not to mention empowering. They give you the sense you're not alone. They provide important data to social media platforms, allowing them to take down accounts and networks engaged in harassment. And they push incremental change forward for other women online.

In the next chapter, we'll discuss the importance of building a community (inclusive of colleagues, friends, family, and employers) that can support you during these moments; they should be your first stop when you're under attack. They may send messages of support or publicly shame platforms into action, and they'll also be around when you need a listening ear. Beyond this inner circle of solidarity, consider reaching out to affinity or membership organizations, labor unions, alumni organizations, and other public bodies with which you are involved. They can post calls to action that will raise awareness about the prevalence of gender-based online hate; such campaigns are especially effective if the organizations also represent men. If you don't have contacts at the social media companies, ask around in these organizations and within your inner circle. Often the best way to get action on content that is clearly violating a platform's terms of service is to get it in front of a human as quickly as possible. Even if a friend of a friend knows someone in the "wrong" department at one of the platforms, often that person can get your report to one of their colleagues more quickly than the official reporting process would. (In the course of writing this chapter, I've reported two accounts impersonating acquaintances to a friend who works at a major platform. Both were taken down within hours after my note. In the past, I have helped friends recover their hacked accounts and even played a role in getting the newly-elected President of Ukraine a verification badge when many impostor accounts floated around online in the days after the 2019 vote. Personal connections matter. I recognize I am lucky and privileged to have them. If you put out a request for help, I and many others like me will do everything we can to put those connections to use. There are also several organizations with crisis help lines in the resources section of this book.)

Ultimately, public support campaigns—whether just a personal post or a much larger and more coordinated effort—inspire action: from platforms, in removing offending content; to communities, who can provide crucial insulation from the most abusive attacks; to bystanders, who hopefully will themselves be inspired to act, reporting and speaking out against these harmful, discriminatory behaviors.

Making Your Case: Law Enforcement

Let me begin with a simple but important statement: I am not a lawyer, nor have I ever filed a police report or sought legal counsel for the online abuse directed at me. Two excellent books—*Hate Crimes in Cyberspace* by Danielle Citron and *Nobody's Victim* by Carrie Goldberg—have informed my knowledge of the legal process surrounding cases of online harassment, cyberstalking, revenge porn, and worse. The authors—both lawyers—lay out how thoroughly inadequate the American legal system is for responding to the unique challenges women face online. (By comparison, Britain has a "Malicious Communications Act, which, among other things, criminalizes trolling meant to deliberately cause 'distress and anxiety.'"[20]) Goldberg has dealt with case after case of clients who sought help from local law enforcement bodies that were usually unaware of the threats of online violence and shockingly ill-equipped to handle them if they were. When Allison Henderson, the victim of a serial SWATter—someone who constantly called in fake threats to send SWAT teams to her home and place of employment—tried to explain her situation to law enforcement, she said "they were completely lost on the idea of a stranger harassing us over the internet. It's feeling like you're drowning, and the person doesn't understand what water is."[21]

You can make the task slightly easier by preparing your evidence before you go to law enforcement or a lawyer. "Documenting and saving the harassment sent to you via Twitter, Facebook, email and other social media can prove useful especially if you decide to pursue legal action and/or report to law enforcement," write Anita Sarkeesian (of the Gamergate scandal), Jaclyn Friedman, and Renee Bracy Sherman.[22] "While local law enforcement are often unfamiliar with online social media, officials recommend that targets report directly threatening online harassment to law enforcement immediately so there is a timely documented record of the abuse." You can do this by snapping a screenshot of the offending content and saving it on your device. Try to include as much information as possible in your screenshot (platform, username, time, date, and engagements), and if you have the time and energy, archive it on the Wayback Machine's Internet Archive (https://web.archive.org/) by inserting the specific web address for the Tweet or post into the "save page now" function. These steps can be a bit cumbersome, especially if you are cataloguing a lot of content or doing so across multiple devices. However, they are probably the best way forward for an average internet user dealing with intermittent or passing threats.

If you have a more serious problem on your hands and resources to throw at it, there's an app (or two) for that. Hunchly is a browser extension that runs in the background as you use the internet, capturing every page you visit as you read it and saving an audit trail. It includes each site's forensic data as well. Marketed to law enforcement, private investigators, and journalists, and priced at $130 per year, Hunchly is a great investment for those that are experiencing sustained abuse. Another similar service, PageVault, comes with a higher price tag and is marketed to lawyers who need court-admissible online evidence.

This does not answer the question of when to report the abuse you're experiencing to law enforcement or seek legal representation. Those are inherently personal choices that I cannot make for you and will vary based on the circumstances of your life and the laws in your jurisdiction. But consider what Danielle Citron writes: "very few women report cyber harassment because they think it is not important enough, the police won't help them, won't take it seriously, or will blame them."[23] But, she argues, given the deficiencies of the legal system, "we should report it whenever we have the resources—monetary, time, human, emotional—to do so." It is an important step in the denormalization of women's treatment online. "Only forty years ago, sexual harassment in the workplace and domestic violence in the home were viewed as normal practices that private individuals had to handle on their own."[24] If we continue to demand solutions—not only from social media, but from our governments—policy change and societal shifts will eventually follow.

After learning about the on-platform tools, avenues of public support you can find, and legal considerations for dealing with gendered abuse and disinformation, I hope you feel more empowered and a lot less alone. We are far from an online utopia, but many of the tools you just learned about did not exist just a few years ago.

When I ask Brianna if she has any parting thoughts for women experiencing online misogyny, she responds, "You don't have to have a *Law and Order* episode written about your life to feel" that what you're going through is stressful, traumatic, or unfair. "Your pain is valid. Don't be shy about getting help. You've gotta have your support group."

And that's exactly what we're discussing next.

TL;DR

1. **Learn about the terms of service and rules on the social media platforms you use,** so when you're hit with abuse and harassment, you know exactly how to report the offending accounts and keep yourself safer.

2. **Mute, block, and report!** These actions don't just make your timeline more bearable, they send important signals to social media platforms about problematic accounts and networks. They can also make certain content less visible to you and your followers.

3. **Take advantage of other on-platform features to make your social media experience less stressful.** Only get notifications for content you care about and for people you know. Turn off replies and comments, and hide or delete offensive responses.

4. If you are self-employed, **consider separating your work and personal emails,** and report abusive messages to email providers.

5. **Reach out to your circle of solidarity—friends, family, colleagues, employers, and affinity organizations—to participate in public support campaigns when you're undergoing attacks.** They can sometimes create a trolling aftershock, but they build awareness and can often shame platforms into action.

6. **Take screenshots of the abuse you receive, or use a tool like Hunchly or PageVault to do so.** This can be helpful for building a case with a lawyer or law enforcement, actions that you should consider if your abuse is severe.

7. **If you have the resources to report your harassment to law enforcement, do so;** you'll be changing the paradigm for the women who come after you.

4

Community: Cultivating a Circle of Solidarity

During every bout of online hate directed at me, my first stop for advice as well as my preferred space to vent has been a Twitter direct message (DM) group of women writers. Talia Lavin, an author and journalist who covers the far right, invited me to join it in 2018. The members are from disparate backgrounds; some cover politics, others write *New York Times*-bestselling fiction or true crime. One is a poetess. What unites us is we are women, and we all write. And that little pocket of the internet, along with a constellation of family, friends, colleagues, and my therapist, have gotten me through the troubling and isolating experiences I have had with angry online mobs.

The women you've met in these pages—Cindy, Nicole, Van, Brianna, and Leta—are all part of the circle of solidarity I've assembled for myself. I first got acquainted with these brilliant, inspiring souls on Twitter. Van and Leta are part of my beloved writer's DM group. Years after I first followed them, we regularly message, amplify each other's work, and if need be, make ourselves available to listen, to act as virtual shoulders to cry on, to celebrate, to hold space for each other's hurt, and to collectively rage. I just met Cindy for the first time in person while writing this book, though we have written articles together, testified to Congress on the same expert panel, and supported each other through the worst of the worst harassment we've received. Nicole and I became acquainted not just because our areas of expertise—the internet and Russia's escapades on it—overlap, but because of online abuse we experience and the solidarity we've shown each other.

Creating this circle of solidarity is not something that happened serendipitously to me; it's part of a very deliberate strategy I continuously implement to build community, camaraderie, and a more equitable, hospitable internet for women, especially those from marginalized communities. Amanda Hess notes, "We use our devices to find supportive communities, make a living, and construct safety nets. [...] The Internet isn't a fun diversion—it is a necessary resource for work and interfacing with friends, family, and, sometimes, law enforcement officers in an effort to feel safer from both online and offline violence."[1]

If you have a public profile, there will be times you need a circle of solidarity to hold you up. There will be times you need to explain to your family members, coworkers, bosses, and even your doctors that you are going through something isolating and frightening and need their help. And on the other end of the spectrum, there will be times where your worst experiences will allow you to support other women going through something similar.

I've always loved the sentiment from the first woman who served as U.S. Secretary of State, Madeleine Albright: "there's a special place in hell for women who don't help each other." (I'd amend Secretary Albright's statement slightly: it would be nice to have an army of men on our side, too.) This chapter is about how to make that happen and make the internet safer for women while you do.

Getting help from family and friends

Creating a safe online environment for yourself can feel like an impossible task. Your closest loved ones likely do not have a public profile. They may not even have social media accounts, or may not use them professionally. How do you explain to them that a bunch of anonymous people on the internet won't leave you alone, or why it bothers you so much? That these strangers are combing through every detail of your life they can find online? That they, your family members and close friends, might be caught in this web of madness, too?

I've found that comparing online abuse to situations in "real life" sometimes helps. "Imagine that every time I walk down the street"—

like in the fictional scenario that opened this book—"a group of men follows me around and makes lewd comments," I'll say. "You wouldn't tell me to 'just ignore' that, right?" Or, more accurately, since the invasion of your online environment can feel much more intimate, personal, and all-consuming than street abuse: "What if I were sitting at my desk, minding my own business, trying to work, while men counted the number of wrinkles on my face, tracked the number of minutes until I reached menopause, or told me to pack it up because writing is a profession better suited to men?"

Even still, your loved ones might not get it, and it won't be particularly productive to relive your abuse to belabor the point. This is where your friends come in. They can be both your shield from further abuse and the soft cocoon of comfort in which you take time away from the world. If your "IRL" friends understand your online life, great! Use them. Ask them very explicitly to help you in some specific way, perhaps by going out together and putting some distance between you and your devices or hanging out and watching trashy TV. Maybe you need a place to stay for a few days if online threats have spilled offline. Whatever the case, I've found that making a discrete request—even if it's just "Can I vent for a few minutes?"—tends to inspire a more helpful response than expressing a vague desire for help.

If your real-life friends are also relatively unreachable, turn to your more wired friends, or friends who are more simpatico with your work and career. Do you have a group of women in your field with whom you share war stories? Message them. Colleagues that you can meet around the water cooler or at happy hour to let off some steam? Meet them. Twitter or Insta or Facebook pals who understand your niche and the specific type of bile you are subjected to? Get on a Zoom call. Your more online friends are also great people to whom you can turn over the keys to your social media, if you just need a break from it all. They can read your notifications, report aggressive, abusive, or violative content, and keep a catalogue of information about the worst offenders so you can keep up your records but not be forced to relive your trauma.

Nicole Perlroth, the *New York Times* journalist who took a break from Twitter, tells me she relied on a small group of colleagues to get her through her toughest moments at the beginning of 2021: "I do have a small Twitter DM group made up of cybersecurity journalists and women in the space who were really supportive," she says. Unfortunately, they were also afraid of inciting a cyber mob: "They took to Twitter from time to time," she tells me, "but also apologized for not doing more because they were too scared." Even so, the solidarity was important. Talia Lavin, who created the DM group that is a huge part of my own support network, relies on her online communities for similar reasons. "It's nice to have people to talk to who unequivocally have your back, especially other public-facing women who have dealt with abuse. People who will call you on crap … but always defend you when it counts, or just empathize during what feels like an incredibly isolating experience."[2]

So how do you find these kindred spirits? It's not as if the first time you log onto a social platform you are automatically ushered into positive, like-minded communities of users. The answer is two-fold; it takes both time and a deliberate engagement strategy to identify and become ingratiated with—or in some cases, build—these communities.

First, spend time curating the accounts with which you interact. Don't be stingy with the follow button; engage with established accounts as much as up-and-comers. It's often in the latter category that you'll find like-minded comrades. But assembling your circle of solidarity isn't only about following people; you must *interact* with them, too. Social media is supposed to be *social*, after all. Typically, I find that women on social media platforms tend to be more passive consumers of information, much more rarely weighing into conversations than their male counterparts (due in no small part, I'm sure, to the abuse that they face online). While I'm not suggesting you become the female equivalent of a reply guy, don't be afraid to weigh in on topics in which you're interested or have expertise! Message people with whom you might have something in common! Make jokes and comment on pictures of people's pets! Or, as Talia says, "reach out to people whose work appeals to your sensibilities and say hello!"

You can also find community in special interest groups and boards. Facebook Groups—while in some cases a notorious source of misinformation—can also provide great networking opportunities. For example, I'm involved in a Women's Foreign Policy Facebook Group, as well as a group for women writers (and, less germane to work, but more germane to joy, groups for alumnae of my college who own dogs or garden). They are excellent places to share joy in recent achievements, get advice, vent, and yes, make friends. Some professions and niches are more focused on anonymous communities like Reddit or Discord. Other groups such as membership-based organizations exist mostly offline, with online components that complement real-life engagement. There, too, you might find fellow travelers. Talia agrees, and says she has found positivity in an often-negative environment. "I like being in community with people from all over the world. It makes me feel less alone and helps create personal, professional, and emotional connection. It shows a much softer and more positive side of the internet, a private kind of deliberate community that can be what you make it."

Building women-friendly online environments

The internet is full of terrible things, but it remains good at connecting people, so long as you expend a little effort. Go one step further and these circles of solidarity can be fortified with patterns of everyday social media engagement that are specifically geared toward building a more women-friendly online environment. It's a tall order given that about two-thirds of users on both Twitter and Reddit are male (Instagram, Facebook, and Tiktok all have gender balances that are truer to life).[3] [4] As Soraya Chemaly notes in *Rage Becomes Her*, "on Twitter, men's tweets are retweeted twice as often as women's."[5]

Here are a few of the conscious practices I keep up to correct these online imbalances:

1. **Follow other women.** Given the gender imbalance on Twitter, I think it's incredibly important to strive toward a more equitable timeline. I follow any woman doing work that is vaguely in my area of interest.
2. **Engage with other women.** Like their content. Share their content. Comment on their content. This tells social media platforms' algorithms that it is high quality and will give it more exposure.
3. Similarly, **if you're sharing content from a man, ask yourself if there is a woman covering the same topic.** Especially on Twitter, when news is breaking, it can be easy to engage with the Tweet with the highest number of interactions. Given the gender breakdown of users on the site, it's likely to be a man. Do a little extra scanning to see if a woman has covered the topic. As an extra bonus, rest easy knowing that women's reporting often represents perspectives their male colleagues may have missed. Let's gas each other up.
4. **Amplify other women.** Be generous in your public support of women around you. There is room out here for all of us. As your finger hovers over the retweet button, imagine Madeline Albright sitting on your shoulder, and consciously choose to avoid that special place in hell.
5. **When you see ongoing harassment, report it, call it out, and send support.** As we've discussed previously, the social platforms get important signals from the reports users send them. If you see an abusive, harassing, or otherwise objectionable piece of content that might be covered by a platform's terms of service, report it. Consider taking a screenshot and calling the behavior out to increase general awareness of the problem among your followers. If a woman you know is undergoing harassment, send her a message of support. She will always appreciate it.

Asking for help from your employers

Online harassment and disinformation campaigns can impact your personal life as well as your career. They can balloon to something much larger than any one person has the capacity to handle. In these cases, it is larger and more influential resources from which we should seek help: professional organizations and employers.

Brittan Heller, a lawyer focusing on online technology and human rights, is intimately aware of how the internet can turn against women. When she was finishing her degree at Yale Law School and applying for jobs, Brittan and Heide Iravani, another woman in her cohort, were the subject of an ongoing campaign of abusive comments on the message board Autoadmit. It claims to be "the most prestigious law school discussion board in the world" for "supporters of the marketplace of ideas and freedom of expression."[6] But as *Washington Post* reporter Ellen Nakashima wrote of the message board in 2007, at the time Brittan was being harassed, Autoadmit also hosts "hundreds of chats posted by anonymous users that feature derisive statements about women, gays, blacks, Asians and Jews. In scores of messages, the users disparage individuals by name or other personally identifying information. Some of the messages included false claims about sexual activity and diseases."[7] As Brittan and her classmate were about to graduate and attempting to find their first post-law school jobs, "the descriptions of them—sluts and whores—and the suggestions about what might be done to them—rape and sodomy—were showing up on Google searches of their names, and had prevented at least one of them from securing employment."[8]

The students decided to bring a federal lawsuit against Autoadmit, suing the message board to reveal the names of those that had defamed them. The case settled out of court, but not before it identified some of the perpetrators. Brittan "was astonished to learn most of them had never met her or had even gone to the same school. They were men and women; professionals and blue-collar workers; young and old."[9] In summer 2021, more than a decade later, Brittan reflected on the case and its repercussions with me. "I'm one of the few people who 'won,'" she says, and that win has impacted her interests in her legal practice.[10] She has worked for the U.S. Department of Justice, the Anti-Defamation League, and the International Criminal

Court, among others. In both her work and her own personal experience, she has observed that employers and other "professional organizations are very ill-equipped to deal with online harassment." After her case against Autoadmit, she says the American Bar Association "decided they were going to create guidelines about looking up job applicants online, the ethics behind that, and if that was a permissible process or not."

But employers need to shoulder more of the burden, Brittan says. "One of the things I'd like to see more of is people engaging on behalf of their employees" who are being harassed "with [those] who can help," such as social media platforms, affinity organizations, or even law firms. Brittan believes this is an important show of solidarity. "It feels like their work cares" about what's happening to them as a result of their work-related public engagement. Journalists are at particular risk, she notes. "I am quite concerned about the way that journalists must be public by nature of their profession and seem to not have a lot of backup from their newsrooms." While some well-resourced publications monitor their employees' social media mentions and pay for privacy protection services like DeleteMe, others leave their journalists to fend for themselves. Freelancers, as well as writers who publish with multiple outlets, find themselves in a much worse situation. "When a journalist writes for one publication and freelances for another as well," says Brittan, "it's not clear who is responsible" for the journalist's safety. "We need to educate people about the scope of assistance that journalists require and the risks that they face." Van Badham, the playwright, activist, and columnist, agrees, and has had to walk her own editors through supporting her during abusive episodes. Van now calls her *Guardian* editor at the earliest inkling of coordinated harassment. "Everybody's learning. What a thing to deal with if you're an editor ... You have a lot on, and you hear 'somebody's being mean to one of our columnists on the internet.' You think 'I have to deal with what now? Where do I even start?'"

Internet users are targeting other industries beyond journalism, as well, Brittan says. "If somebody makes a false review of your business on Yelp or a disgruntled employee puts a post up on [the recruitment site] Indeed, or on Rate My Doctor, those are not a regulated space." Those professional spheres lack clear guidance about what can be career-ending online defamation.

What *is* clear, however, is that employers need help getting up to speed and protecting their public-facing employees, particularly women and those with intersectional identities. In most cases, it will likely fall to employees to mount a campaign with an organization's leadership to protect those who might endure online abuse. If you're in this position, you should consider the following steps to build an institutional policy.

First, spell out the problem. Ideally this step occurs before someone at the organization is targeted online, using the wide body of research available (consider showing leadership this book, and consult the resources section at the back for further reading). If someone—or multiple employees—in your organization has already experienced online abuse, gather screenshots of the campaigns (which you've been collecting since you read the previous chapter, right?) and show executives, board members, or other power players what happened. Estimate the time and expenses you have outlaid in responding to the abuse, as well as how it has affected your ability to do your job.

Then, request the creation of a new policy on online harassment. In the twenty-first century, most organizations have developed policies on social media, laying out what employees can and cannot say and do online. Generally, these policies are there to protect employers from embarrassment; most don't realize that embarrassment and negative attention can materialize even when their employees do everything "right," in the form of online harassment campaigns. The natural corollary to a social media posting policy is an institutional policy that also protects employees from online harms. Defector Media, a sports reporting and commentary website, dedicates an entire section of their Human Resources policy to dealing with online harassment.[11] "Defector will support you as best as we possibly can if you are facing a period of intense and/or sustained online harassment," it reads. Every Defector employee has a precautionary subscription to DeleteMe, which can be upgraded to "white glove service" during severe campaigns. Employees can choose to have a colleague take over their social media presence, and Defector will pay for up to ten days of relocation if an employee feels unsafe in their home and encourages targets of abuse to take time off work under their sick leave policy. Finally, the organization provides its employees with legal and emotional support and will assist them in working with law enforcement if desired.

Outside of policies to support victims of online harassment, executives and leaders also have a special responsibility to implement no-tolerance policies for harassers themselves. Nicole Perlroth noticed she was receiving a lot of abuse from employees of a single cybersecurity company. "A lot of [the messages] seemed to come from people who probably hang out on the same Slack channel. It doesn't reflect well on the company," Nicole said. She had been in touch with the CEO previously, so she messaged him and expressed her frustration. "CEOs should get called out when their employees form online mob groups," she told me. "They should be telling people 'watch the general tenor of your social media interactions.' If you're constantly dismissing something a woman says ... maybe that's not okay." The abuse stopped once she got in touch with the CEO.

Creating a supportive environment in the office and its online extension is not only an emotional and psychological boost for employees actively undergoing harassment; it builds the circumstances in which women, who often preemptively self-censor in anticipation of online abuse, can feel safer to publicly express themselves. When women know their employers have our backs, we write the story that might bring out violent fringe groups. We pursue the research that challenges long-standing power structures. We are less afraid to say the things that might make men mad. In short, we are able to more equitably participate in public discourse. That's the power that employers have if they choose to recognize and use it.

An Ode to Therapy

As I've mentioned, during the worst of the abuse I received in 2020, it sometimes felt like my family and friends didn't understand what I was going through. I was isolated and exhausted from feeling like I constantly had to explain why I was so upset. Worse, I was afraid to wear out my loved ones who *did* get it by incessantly rehashing my frustration and anger at the perpetrators of the abuse.

Thank God for my therapist. She has seen me through the development of my public profile, from my first major publication to the writing of this manuscript. ("Remember that you are strong and that you are writing this book not only because it is a passion project but because it is needed within our incredibly messed up culture," she wrote to me as I was finishing the draft.) When I first told her about the online abuse I was experiencing, I downplayed it a little. "Just some crazy people on the internet who have nothing better to do with their time but harass me," I laughed. "I didn't get anything *so* bad. No rape threats, and I haven't been doxxed yet." But as I continued to tell her about the experience, my true emotions bubbled up. I was upset. I felt wronged and helpless. At the same time, I was wondering if I was overreacting. My therapist helped me acknowledge that my reactions were not only valid, they were normal and not an overreaction in the slightest. If I wanted to discuss every last one of the abusive tweets I was sent, she would be happy to do so.

Other women I interviewed for this book also value therapy. Nicole Perlroth told me that it has been incredibly helpful for her. After a particularly difficult review of her book by a man who Nicole felt was willfully misunderstanding her work because of her gender and lack of technical bona fides, "I put my computer down and I went to my therapist and read him the review," she told me. Her therapist said: "You know what that is Nicole? That is a bruised male ego." Brianna Wu thinks therapy was integral to her channeling her experience into activism. Soraya Chemaly, the author of *Rage Becomes Her*, includes therapy as part of her step-by-step plan to productively channel your rage:

The day I published my first article, I made an appointment to see a therapist. She was smart, caring, and compassionate. Through long discussions with her over a period of years, the way I thought about anger and myself shifted. Weathering the vicissitudes of being a Woman on the Internet, on the receiving end of a perpetual stream of ugliness, would have been infinitely more difficult if I hadn't been able to do this.[12]

Chemaly recognizes—as do I—that therapy is integral to our contributions to a world set up against us. But therapy is not always accessible; in some countries, like the United Kingdom and many Eastern European nations, seeking therapy is looked down upon, viewed as "paying someone to listen to you whinge." (I am sad to admit this is a real quote from an English friend, though in recent years this attitude appears to be shifting.) In the United States, therapy is incredibly expensive, and few therapists are "in-network" with American health insurers, meaning you must go through extra steps to get reimbursed for sessions that can run upwards of $200 out of pocket. If cost is an obstacle to starting therapy for you, ask your therapist if she has a sliding fee scale. Explore options that are in-network with your insurance provider. Understand the out-of-pocket reimbursement practices. If you're on a university campus, health centers usually offer students and staff access to psychological support services; U.S. states also offer publicly-funded mental health programs. Explore group therapy, too; it might be a place for you to expand your circle of solidarity. I had these and other impediments to beginning a relationship with a therapist, too, but I'm so thankful I worked through them. My sessions have made the most difficult moments of my public-facing career much more bearable.

Part of what online abusers hope to achieve is to make you feel alone. They hope that you'll feel so isolated you will judge your public engagement not worth the consequences they've attempted to impose on you. Your circle of solidarity is there to remind you that you're not alone, that it's worth engaging, that the world needs your voice, and that they're around to support you. In a way, even the less-than-comforting interactions I've had with family and friends who can't identify with what I'm going through have motivated me to speak up and speak more loudly than ever before; there are so many people out there—including some very close to me—who need to hear what I have to say and who could benefit from a widening of the aperture on their understanding of women's online experiences.

More importantly, though, supporting each other makes all our online experiences a little kinder and easier. During the COVID-19 pandemic, I began mentoring early-career women over Zoom. (You don't need any special qualifications to be a mentor, so I encourage you to do it too. It benefits both mentor and mentee and creates more online and offline solidarity for women of all ages.) About half of them asked me for advice about dealing with online harassment. They wanted to know how I survived it, how to stop it, and how to respond when—not if—it happened to them. These conversations were not only an important part of building a better online environment for young women, but of expanding their circles of solidarity. Every woman who asked that question can help others in the future. They will amplify their friends and follow other women on Twitter. They will call out abuse when they see it. They will advocate for better policies on supporting targets of online harassment within their organizations. They will, if possible, seek therapy so they can most effectively channel their anger. And, little by little, moment by moment, tweet by tweet, they will build a more equitable environment not only for themselves and their peers, but for the women who come after them, too.

TL;DR

1. **Lean on your family and friends.** Try to explain what you're going through and make explicit asks for support.
2. **Build and engage a circle of online friends who "get it."** Your friends and family may not always come through, but other women and colleagues in your area of expertise or field may have a better

idea of what you're going through. Actively seek out those communities *before* you're in crisis.

3. **Engage in online practices that make the internet safer and more equitable for women.** Follow and engage with women. Amplify their work. Report harassment and send messages of support.

4. **Pressure and work with your employers to craft sensible policies for employees undergoing online abuse,** particularly if your job requires external engagement.

5. **Get a therapist.** If cost is an obstacle, explore sliding-scale options, group therapy, or publicly-funded care. Having someone to unabashedly speak to about your experiences is invaluable.

5

Tenacity: Speaking Up and Fighting Back

You've now read over 25,000 words of tips and advice on how to protect yourself online and fight back against those who wish to silence you. But the system is still stacked against us. In large part, men built social media platforms for the world that *they* inhabit. Just like some of our more analog family and friends have trouble understanding what our digital lives are like and the impact they have on us offline, the men who built these systems generally cannot fathom what it would be like to have an online fan become an offline stalker. They can't imagine the precautions women must take to protect themselves online, because they do not have the same considerations. And sometimes, they even use the systems they helped build to harass and abuse women themselves.

In the first chapter of their tell-all book about Facebook, *New York Times* journalists Sheera Frenkel and Cecilia Kang reveal that Facebook engineers were using the platform's internal systems to access private user data. "Nearly every month, engineers had exploited the tools designed to give them easy access to data for building new products to violate the privacy of Facebook users and infiltrate their lives," they write.[1] "Men who looked up the Facebook profiles of women they were interested in made up the vast majority" of the 52 engineers fired for abusing their data access privileges from January 2014 to August 2015.[2] One man tracked his estranged girlfriend after she left him; another used private user data to stalk a woman he was scheduled to meet for a date. He approached her in a park where she was meeting her friends.

It is not just social media platforms that face challenges of systemic online inequality; on Wikipedia, the online encyclopedia, only 19 percent of its 1.5 million biographies are of women.[3] "Women in all fields are underrepresented, articles about women's interests are underdeveloped, and women are less likely to edit Wikipedia articles," writes Francesca Tripodi in a study of gender and representation on the platform.[4] The inequality is systemic: "the interpretation and application of Wikipedia's notability guidelines play a critical role in the perpetuation of gender inequality on the site ... Biographies about women who meet Wikipedia's criteria for inclusion are more likely to be considered non-notable than men's."[5] This impacts public perceptions of women's contributions to society, as well as results on search engines like Google.

The search giant itself has had its own struggles with gender and racial inequality. In late 2020, Google fired Timnit Gebru, "one of the most high-profile Black women in her field and a powerful voice in the new field of ethical AI, which seeks to identify issues around bias, fairness, and responsibility."[6] She sought to publish a paper exploring the ethical risks of large language models, a technology on which Google relies, and which could have effects on marginalized communities. Her employer asked her to retract her co-authorship of the paper. According to Gebru, when she asked for more transparency around the company's review process, she was fired. Google claimed she resigned. For months after her dismissal, she was incessantly harassed on Twitter.[7] "Some [anonymous users] called Gebru a bitch and told her to 'go back to Africa.' Others said she was arrogant and only hired at Google because she is Black."[8]

The infrastructure of the internet is built *for* men and *with* men's safety in mind. But even among women, there are different planes of online abuse. Women of intersectional identities, representing additional marginalized groups—such as race, ethnicity, sexual orientation and physical ability—are subject to higher and more intense levels of harassment, attacking multiple aspects of their personhood. The concept of "intersectionality" has become the bogeyman of the far right and critics of so-called "cancel culture," but it must be at the core of our understanding of the online environment in our quest for a more equitable internet.

The term "intersectional feminism" was coined by Kimberlé Crenshaw in 1989. More than 30 years later, she told TIME magazine that today, intersectionality is:

> *a lens, a prism, for seeing the way in which various forms of inequality often operate together and exacerbate each other. We tend to talk about race inequality as separate from inequality based on gender, class, sexuality or immigrant status. What's often missing is how some people are subject to all of these.*[9]

UN Women, which works toward gender equality and women's empowerment, calls intersectionality "a framework through which to build inclusive, robust movements that work to solve overlapping forms of discrimination, simultaneously."[10] In short, intersectionality is not about undermining a specific gender, race, or class; it is about increasing equality for all. As Crenshaw noted to TIME, even in the 2020s, "the image of the citizen is still a male citizen. When you get to a few gender topics—like reproductive rights—then we talk about women. But politics and policy are pretty much like medicine used to be and still is: the male body is the body." And it is intersectional bodies that are the victims of this system, online and off.

Shireen Mitchell, the founder of Stop Online Violence Against Women and a tireless advocate for equality both online and offline, told a Wilson Center focus group about her own experience as a Black woman in the technology sector and the layered harassment she has experienced:

> *There is sexual stuff that happens, or things that are based on our gender, but women of color deal with both the gender harassment perspectives, in addition to the racial aspects that come at us. And, sometimes, they're right on top of each other, and layered on top of each other, without people understanding what's happening."*[11]

Shireen noted that content moderators at social media platforms, not to mention those setting platform policy itself, do not understand the unique threats that Black women and other women with intersectional identities receive. She discussed how Leslie Jones, a

Black, female comedian, was abused on Twitter, but the platform responded too slowly. "People didn't realize that putting Harambe, a dead gorilla's face, on her body was a death threat," Shireen said. "They had no concept of the understanding of calling us apes and then putting a dead gorilla on her head was a death threat with an image." Black women's families are often threatened, she underlined. They are told "I hope your child doesn't become a hashtag." Abusers send pizzas to their home addresses as a warning: "we know where you live."

These tactics affect other women of color, transgender women and other members of the LGBTQ community, and disabled women. As my own research has shown, the most popular narratives of gendered disinformation against women in public life are sexual, racist, or transphobic in nature.[12] Women from marginalized communities experience more and categorically worse abuse than their non-marginalized counterparts. The abuse often spills over to offline violence. The threats women with intersectional identities experience are pernicious. They are abhorrent. And until we address them as the intersectional problems they are, the wider problem of online abuse against women will not be solved. As civil rights activist Fannie Lou Hamer told the National Women's Political Caucus at its inaugural meeting, in a speech about the struggle of Black feminists, "nobody's free until everybody's free."[13]

Achieving that freedom is impossible if we stay silent. Silence is a norm we simply cannot afford to accept. I realized this with the help of a good friend when I was living in Ukraine. As an advisor to the country's Ministry of Foreign Affairs, I was working every day alongside brilliant women who bore the burden of Ukrainian society's expectations of them. Not only were they skilled diplomats and press attachés; they were mothers and caretakers. In addition to their high-pressure jobs, they cooked and cleaned at home and organized office parties and other social events at work. They were also expected to be physically impeccable at all times. Their makeup, hair, nails, shoes (high heels, always), and outfits were a level of perfection I could only have achieved with a full-time team at my beck and call.

Beyond societal expectations, the work environment in Ukraine is not an easy one for women. Female role models among the upper echelons of Ukrainian government were few. My boss at the Ministry was Mariana Betsa, the spokesperson and one of the highest-ranking women in the building. We were regularly the only women in meetings. At one contentious gathering, after the men hobnobbed and shook each other's hands (but never ours, a gendered relic of Soviet culture) the discussion got heated. Another advisor to the Ministry, the only other Westerner in the room, who happened to be an older man, actively shushed her, pounding on the table. I was appalled and upset, but as the youngest person in the room, not to mention a foreign woman, I did not feel empowered to say anything.

Months later, the same Western advisor and I had a meeting with Mariana. As we prepared for an upcoming training that would involve a role-playing exercise for press officers, he suggested I play "that bitch from the *Wall Street Journal.*" Again, I said nothing in the moment. I was focused on getting the job done and the meeting finished, but I mentioned the offensive phrase to a male colleague and close friend later. Only when I saw his shock and distaste did I allow myself to truly be angry. He encouraged me to report the other advisor because his behavior—even absent the context of advising a highly traditional and misogynistic government while actively engaging in and tacitly condoning some of its worst practices—was unacceptable even under the most forgiving interpretations.

I escalated a paragraphs-long complaint through diplomatic channels. The outcome—a mealy-mouthed apology from the higher-ups involved, and awkward avoidance from the perpetrator—was not satisfying personally. But the experience was an important lesson for me professionally. In elementary school, I hadn't been afraid to peck my first-grade classmate in the face with my bird mask on Halloween. He had disrespected me, and I let him know it. Until the incident in Ukraine, that spirit had not translated to my professional life. And until

I started receiving sexualized abuse on the internet, that spirit hadn't powered my professional presence online, either.

With so much of modern life lived on social media, email, messaging apps, and Zoom, unless we continue to protect ourselves, speak up, and fight back—not only for ourselves, but for the women around us who may not enjoy our societal privileges—we are actively forfeiting the latest frontier in the struggle for gender equality. As Laura Bates, the founder of the Everyday Sexism Project, told Soraya Chemaly in *Rage Becomes Her*, many women think "this is the way things are. This is what it means to be a woman. I just have to deal with" constant abuse, whether at work, school, online, or walking through a park to get home at night. "It wasn't until I realized this is a collective experience that I began to feel anger."[14] For me, it wasn't until I was upset on behalf of my Ukrainian colleagues *and* a trusted male colleague validated my indignation that I felt I could voice that anger.

Now that I recognize it, I refuse to be silenced about our collective experience of harassment, abuse, and inequity, online or off. I will not surrender my voice, not only because I wholeheartedly decline to give @ProfessorActuallyEsq, @TrojanHorace, @LazyLogan and all their friends the satisfaction of victory, but because each of us have an important role to play in increasing awareness of physical and online security, helping our peers endure adversity, working to change policy, and building community. We have a collective tenacity that, if activated, can challenge the norms that so many have written off as an unfortunate but immutable characteristic of women's online engagement.

I am committed to harnessing that tenacity with every tweet, every TikTok, every keystroke, and every click.

I will continue to invest in the time-consuming and sometimes-expensive practices, where my resources allow, to enable myself and others to speak out.

I will recognize that my timeline is a queendom, not a democracy, and mute, block, and report as much as I see necessary.

I will familiarize myself with platform policy and use it to create a more equitable online environment.

I will build a circle of solidarity that is inclusive and supportive, committed to amplifying other women.

I will seek help from friends, family, colleagues, and professionals when I need it.

I will be unshakeable, calling out the unacceptable behaviors, policies, and infrastructures that enable harassment.

I will do this not only for myself, but for all women, especially those facing intersectional, layered threats.

I will do this because the internet is a critical public space for discussion, politics, activism, and expression. Until women—all women, no matter their race, sexual identity, religion, or ability—have an equal voice there, we aren't truly equal anywhere. If the United States can elect its first female Vice President and witness the appointment of more women in Cabinet positions and Congress than ever before, but these women are regularly lambasted with sexual epithets, we haven't achieved the equality we project.

You can help us get there. Maybe before you read this book you had already experienced abuse and wanted to know how to better protect yourself. Maybe you knew little about how women are targeted online and wanted to learn how to be a better ally. Either way, keep speaking up. Keep fighting back. This is how, together, we can make it healthier, safer, and easier to be a woman online.

Further Reading

A list of crucial research and writing that has shaped my understanding of this problem. For even more information, see this book's endnotes.

Books

Rage Becomes Her: The Power of Women's Anger, by Soraya Chemaly (Atria, 2018)

Hate Crimes in Cyberspace, by Danielle Citron (Harvard University Press, 2014)

Nobody's Victim: Fighting Psychos, Stalkers, Pervs, and Trolls, by Carrie Goldberg (Penguin Random House, 2019)

The Internet of Garbage, by Sarah Jeong (Vox Media, 2018)

Credible Threat: Attacks Against Women Online and the Future of Democracy, by Sarah Sobieraj (Oxford University Press, 2020)

This is Why We Can't Have Nice Things: Mapping the Relationship Between Online Trolling and Mainstream Culture, Whitney Phillips (The MIT Press, 2016)

Articles and Policy Papers

"No Excuse for Abuse," PEN America 2021

"Attacks and Harassment: The Impact on Female Journalists and Their Reporting," the International Women's Media Foundation, 2018

"Bringing Women, Peace and Security Online: Mainstreaming Gender in Responses to Online Extremism," Alexis Heneshaw, Global Network on Extremism and Technology, 2021

"Online violence Against Women Journalists: A Global Snapshot of Incidence and Impacts," Julie Posetti et al, UNESCO, 2021

"FREE TO BE ONLINE? A report on girls' and young women's experiences of online harassment," PLAN International, 2020

"Engendering Hate: The Contours of State-Aligned Gendered Disinformation Online," NDI and Demos, 2021

Resources

The following resources are provided as recommendations for those looking for resources and support. They do not necessarily constitute endorsements of specific products or services, but are meant to help you on your journey to speaking up and fighting back.

- **Navigating platform policies:** When I was working on gendered harassment and disinformation at the Wilson Center, one of my brilliant interns, Zoë Kaufmann, put together a chart of social media platform policies on violence, abuse, harassment, targeted harassment, and coordinated abuse. Contained at the back of our "Malign Creativity" report, it is a one stop shop for learning more about how platforms' policies inform their responses to the abuse you experience. Using it will help you navigate the reporting process more smoothly. https://www.wilsoncenter.org/publication/malign-creativity-how-gender-sex-and-lies-are-weaponized-against-women-online
- **Anti-Doxing Subscriptions:** As discussed in Chapter One, anti-doxing services remove your personal information like your address, phone number, and other critical data from aggregator websites. Below are the services many of my peers use.
  - DeleteMe by Abine: joindeleteme.com
  - Reputation Defender: reputationdefender.com
- **Evidence cataloguing:** If you are looking for a way to seamlessly capture and store screenshots of the abuse against you or your research into the perpetrators of said abuse, the services below offer ways to save such data. Page Vault is admissible in court.
  - Hunchly: hunch.ly
  - Page Vault: page-vault.com
- **Two-Factor Authentication (2FA):** Using 2FA is a must for securing your accounts. You can do this through mobile applications like those listed below. For a physical security key, try Yubikey.

- – Duo Mobile: duo.com/product/multi-factor-authentication-mfa/duo-mobile-app
  - – LastPass Authenticator: lastpass.com/auth/
  - – Authy: authy.com
  - – Google Authenticator: search in the app store on your device
  - – Microsoft Authenticator: microsoft.com/en-us/account/authenticator
- **Virtual Private Networks (VPNs):** Ensure that your internet traffic cannot be viewed by anyone snooping on you.
  - – ExpressVPN: expressvpn.com
  - – Surfshark: surfshark.com
  - – NordVPN: nordvpn.com
  - – ProtonVPN: protonvpn.com
  - – IPVanish: ipavanish.com
  - – TunnelBear: tunnelbear.com
- **Encrypted messengers and email services:** Ensure that only your intended recipient reads the messages you send them.
  - – Signal (encrypted private messenger): signal.org
  - – ProtonMail (encrypted email service): protonmail.com
- **Password Managers:** Password managers keep your passwords complex and secure. It's best not to use the native password managers on your web browser or single-sign-on through your Google, Facebook, or Amazon account as an attacker who gained access to one of your umbrella accounts would then be able to access all the accounts connected to that service. HaveIBeenPwned.com and HaveIBeenZucked.com offer databases of most recent hacks (as well as Facebook data breaches), so you can check the relative security of your accounts and change your password if necessary. Some reliable password managers include those listed below. Reading tech blogs to compare the services and see how experts rate them is always helpful before committing to a single service.
  - – LastPass: lastpass.com
  - – 1Password: 1password.com

- BitWarden: bitwarden.com
- Dashlane: dashlane.com
- **Social media and trolling management:** If you want help managing trolls and abusers, Block Party can help. As of publication, the service is only available for Twitter, but plans to expand in the future. You can add yourself to the waiting list for free or pay $8 for instant access. blockpartyapp.com

- Support Networks: this is not a complete list of the organizations dedicated to online abuse, though these are some of the resources I have consulted myself.
  - **The Online Violence Response Hub** (onlineviolenceresponsehub.org): created by the International Women's Media Foundation and the International Coalition for Female Journalists, "is a robust resource center where women journalists – and newsrooms – can find updated research, emergency assistance, and easy-to-follow recommendations for their specific situation."
  - **Crash Override Network** (crashoverridenetwork.com): an advocacy group and resource center for those experiencing online abuse, led by Zoë Quinn, one of the targets of Gamergate.
  - **Glitch UK** (glitchcharity.co.uk): a UK-based charity that does campaigns, training, and advocacy to "make the internet a safer place for everyone."

Acknowledgments

I didn't think I would begin another manuscript less than a year after my first book was published. When well-meaning friends and colleagues asked if I had plans for a second book, I would jokingly respond, "Is that a threat?" But writing this book—despite the dark subject matter—has been a joy. Having experienced online abuse myself, and having steeped myself in the facts of the phenomenon that so many women quietly face, it helped to orient me toward change. I know that—like the women's suffrage movement and the women's liberation movement and all the hard-fought battles that we've won for centuries—we can upset the norms currently governing how women are treated online. I believe this book can be a small part of that.

I am hugely grateful to all the women who have shared their stories with me. In this book, you've met: Van Badham, Brittan Heller, Leta Hong Fincher, Talia Lavin, Shireen Mitchell, Cindy Otis, Nicole Perlroth, and Brianna Wu. They are warriors, and I'm so grateful to be in the trenches with them, to have them in my life, and to learn from them. To the young women and experts who participated in online focus groups to inform my thinking and research, thank you for sharing your time and experience. And to my incredible team on the Wilson Center's "Malign Creativity" project—Jillian Hunchak, Celia Davies, Alexa Pavliuc, Shannon Pierson, Zoë Kaufmann, Micah Clark, and Clyde Seto—whose dogged and incisive work was the basis of the landmark report that inspired this book: thank you for the impactful and incredibly important contributions you made to the international conversation about gendered abuse and disinformation.

To my early readers, Ryan Beiermeister and Courtney Callejas, thank you for making sure I didn't embarrass myself in this text, and for your encouragement in assuring me this book helped you and could help others.

To my editor at Bloomsbury, Tomasz Hoskins, who brought this idea out and encouraged its fruition: what a pleasure to know I have a trusted friend and colleague like you in my corner. Thank you.

To Pete Kiehart, for encouraging me to go for it and for always being around to hash out existential crises, not to mention for his very excellent photographs.

To Holly Donaldson, Alexa Pavliuc, Sabra Ayres, Emily Rodriguez, Cindy Otis, Courtney Callejas, Emily Malina, Rae Jean Stokes, Melissa Hooper, the Grotto, and the other strong women who hold me up—not an easy job during a pandemic when in-person contact is limited—I don't think I'd have gotten through this year without you.

To my mom, the original strong woman in my life. I'm so lucky to have had you and Dad to teach me to assert myself and to continue to have your support and encouragement.

To my husband, Mike, who has now put up with the completion of two manuscripts—and the fugue states that come along with them—in two years: you are a saint. Thank you for your judgement-free support and love, and for cleaning Baxter's litter box and walking Jake when I'm in a heap on the couch. I love you.

About the Author

Nina Jankowicz is an internationally-recognized expert on disinformation and democratization. Her debut book, *How to Lose the Information War*, was named a *New Statesman* 2020 book of the year; *The New Yorker* called it "a persuasive new book on disinformation as a geopolitical strategy."

Jankowicz's expertise spans the public, private, and academic sectors. She has advised governments, international organizations, and tech companies; testified before the U.S. Congress, UK Parliament, and European Parliament; and led accessible, actionable research about the effects of disinformation on women, minorities, democratic activists, and freedom of expression around the world.

Jankowicz has extensive media experience, with writing published in major newspapers and magazines and regular appearances on flagship radio and television programs. Since 2017, she has held fellowships at the Wilson Center in Washington, DC. In 2016–2017, Jankowicz advised the Ukrainian Foreign Ministry on disinformation and strategic communications under the auspices of a Fulbright-Clinton Public Policy Fellowship.

Jankowicz holds a Master's degree from Georgetown University's School of Foreign Service. She is a proud alumna of Bryn Mawr College, where she studied Political Science and Russian and graduated magna cum laude.

Notes

Introduction

1 Danielle Citron, *Hate Crimes in Cyberspace*, (Cambridge: Harvard University Press, 2014), 74–80.

2 Sarah Jeong, *The Internet of Garbage*. The Verge/Vox Media, Inc, version 1.5, 2018. 19. https://cdn.vox-cdn.com/uploads/chorus_asset/file/12599893/The_Internet_of_Garbage.0.pdf

3 Cécile Guerin and Eisha Maharasingam-Shah, "Public Figures, Public Rage: Candidate Abuse on Social Media," The Institute for Strategic Dialogue, 2020. 3–4. https://www.isdglobal.org/wp-content/uploads/2020/10/Public-Figures-Public-Rage-4.pdf

4 Julie Posetti et al, "Online Violence Against Women Journalists: A Global Snapshot of Incidence and Impacts," UNESCO, 2021, 2. https://www.icfj.org/sites/default/files/2020-12/UNESCO%20Online%20Violence%20Against%20Women%20Journalists%20-%20A%20Global%20Snapshot%20Dec9pm.pdf

5 Nina Jankowicz et al, "Malign Creativity: How Gender, Sex, and Lies are Weaponized Against Women Online," The Wilson Center, 25 January 2021, 1. https://www.wilsoncenter.org/sites/default/files/media/uploads/documents/Report%20Malign%20Creativity%20How%20Gender%2C%20Sex%2C%20and%20Lies%20are%20Weaponized%20Against%20Women%20Online_0.pdf

6 Michelle P. Ferrier, "Attacks and Harassment: The Impact on Female Journalists and Their Reporting," 7. http://www.IWMF/TrollBusters, 2018, iwmf.org/wp-content/uploads/2018/09/Attacks-and-Harassment.pdf

7 Kristen Zeiter et al, "Tweets that Chill: Analyzing Online Violence Against Women in Politics," The National Democratic Institute, 14 June 2019, 19–20. https://www.ndi.org/sites/default/files/NDI%20Tweets%20That%20Chill%20Report.pdf

8 Helen Lewis, "'You should have your tongue ripped out': the reality of sexist abuse online," *New Statesman*, 3 November 2011. https://www.

newstatesman.com/blogs/helen-lewis-hasteley/2011/11/comments-rape-abuse-women

9 Jankowicz et al, 41.

10 Author focus group with college students. Virtual. 23 June 2021.

11 Sharon Gould et al, "Free to Be Online? Girls' and Young Women's Experiences of Online Harassment," Plan International, 2020. 16. https://plan-international.org/publications/freetobeonline

12 Ibid., 31.

13 Ibid.

1 Security: Outfitting Yourself Online

1 Author interview with Cindy Otis. Virtual. 24 June 2021.

2 Ryan Grenoble, "Rep. Mo Brooks Responds To Lawsuit By Accidentally Sharing Email Password," *The Huffington Post,* 7 June 2021. https://www.huffpost.com/entry/mo-brooks-lawsuit-email-password_n_60be38e5e4b0882193c711c8

3 Brian Barrett, "Sorry, But Your Browser Password Manager Probably Isn't Enough," WIRED, 30 August 2016. https://www.wired.com/2016/08/browser-password-manager-probably-isnt-enough/

4 Jason Koebler, "Basic Digital Security Could Have Prevented One of the Biggest Political Scandals in American History," *Vice,* 13 July 2018. https://www.vice.com/en/article/ywkd35/two-factor-authentication-russia-hacking-indictment

5 TunnelBear, "What is a VPN?: 2021 Guide," TunnelBear.com, 2021. https://www.tunnelbear.com/what-is-vpn

6 Rae Hodge, David Gewirtz, "Best VPN service of 2021," CNET, 29 June 2021. https://www.cnet.com/news/best-vpn/

7 Ibid.

8 Edith Ramirez et al, "Data Brokers: A Call for Transparency and Accountability," US Federal Trade Commission, May 2014. B-3 - B-6. https://www.ftc.gov/system/files/documents/reports/data-brokers-call-transparency-accountability-report-federal-trade-commission-may-2014/140527databrokerreport.pdf

9 Bruce Schneier, "Doxing as an Attack," *Schneier on Security*, 2 January 2015. https://www.schneier.com/blog/archives/2015/01/doxing_as_an_at.html

10 Jeong, *The Internet of Garbage*, 26.

11 Ibid., 28.

12 Lyz Lenz, "When the Mob Comes," *Men Explain Things To Me*, 31 March 2021. https://lyz.substack.com/p/when-the-mob-comes

13 See DeleteMe's free opt-out guide: https://joindeleteme.com/help/diy-free-opt-out-guide/

2 Adversity: Enduring Trolls

1 https://twitter.com/nicoleperlroth/status/1365356748110897152?s=20

2 https://twitter.com/nicoleperlroth/status/1365359531513974786?s=20

3 Author interview with Nicole Perlroth, virtual, 21 October 2020.

4 Author interview with Nicole Perlroth, phone, 15 June 2021.

5 https://twitter.com/nicoleperlroth/status/1365380868949204993

6 Author interview with Van Badham, virtual, 30 June 2021.

7 https://www.aihw.gov.au/reports/domestic-violence/family-domestic-sexual-violence-in-australia-2018/summary

8 https://www.abc.net.au/news/2016-07-12/my-ovaries-made-me-trends-on-twitter-after-q&a-spat/7589942

9 Soraya Chemaly, *Rage Becomes Her: The Power of Women's Anger*. (New York: Atria, 2018). 215.

10 Chemaly, 161–2.

11 Van Badham, "Twitter, the barbarian country, or how I learned to love the block button," *The Guardian*, 30 January 2019. https://www.theguardian.com/commentisfree/2019/jan/31/twitter-the-barbarian-country-or-how-i-learned-to-love-the-block-button

12 Chemaly, 151.

13 Ibid., 178.

14 Badham, "Twitter, the barbarian country."

15 Anna Kramer, "What Tracy Chou learned about online harassment while building an app to solve it," *Protocol*, 26 January 2021. https://www.protocol.com/harassment-block-party-app

3 Policy: Making it Work for You

1 Brianna Wu, "I'm Risking My Life Standing Up To Gamergate," *Bustle*, 11 February 2015. https://www.bustle.com/articles/63466-im-brianna-wu-and-im-risking-my-life-standing-up-to-gamergate

2 Charlie Warzel, "How an Online Mob Created a Playbook for a Culture War," *The New York Times*, 15 August 2019. https://www.nytimes.com/interactive/2019/08/15/opinion/what-is-gamergate.html

3 Jim Franklin, "A Difficult Situation," SendGrid.Com, 21 March 2013. https://sendgrid.com/blog/a-difficult-situation/

4 Author interview with Brianna Wu, virtual, 18 June 2021.

5 Brianna Wu, "I Wish I Could Tell You It's Gotten Better. It Hasn't.," *The New York Times*, 15 August 2019. https://www.nytimes.com/interactive/2019/08/15/opinion/brianna-wu-gamergate.html

6 Steve LeBlanc, "Once the target of online threats, gaming engineer plans run for Congress," PBS Newshour, 23 December 2016. https://www.pbs.org/newshour/politics/online-threats-gaming-engineer-plans-run-congress

7 Author interview with Leta Hong Fincher. Phone. 23 October 2020.

8 Adapted from Jankowicz et al, "Malign Creativity," The Wilson Center.

9 https://twitter.com/LetaHong/status/1295423971853312002?s=20

10 Sarah Sobieraj, Credible Threat: Attacks Against Women Online and the Future of Democracy (Oxford University Press, 2020). 110.

11 The World Wide Web Foundation, "Facebook, Google, TikTok and Twitter make unprecedented commitments to tackle the abuse of women on their platforms," 1 July 2021. https://webfoundation.org/2021/07/generation-equality-commitments/

12 https://twitter.com/settings/notifications/filters

13 Twitter, "About Replies and Mentions." https://help.twitter.com/en/using-twitter/mentions-and-replies

14 Jarrod Doherty, "Introducing Safety Mode," Twitter.com, 1 September 2021. https://blog.twitter.com/en_us/topics/product/2021/introducing-safety-mode

15 https://www.facebook.com/privacy/checkup

16 https://www.facebook.com/journalist_registration

17 https://www.google.com/gmail/about/policy/

18 PBS Newshour, "#Gamergate leads to death threats against women in the gaming industry," PBS Newshour, 16 October 2014. https://www.pbs.org/newshour/show/gamergate-leads-death-threats-women

19 Coalition for Women in Journalism, "China: CFWIJ Stands with Journalist Leta Hong Fincher Who Has Been the Target of Misogynist Trolling," 20 July 2020. https://womeninjournalism.org/cfwij-press-statements/china-cfwij-stands-with-journalist-leta-hong-fincher-who-has-been-the-target-of-misogynistic-trolling

20 Carrie Goldberg and Jeannine Amber, *Nobody's Victim: Fighting Psychos, Stalkers, Pervs, and Trolls* (Plume: 2019), 144.

21 Jason Fagone, "The Serial Swatter," *The New York Times Magazine*, 24 November 2015. https://www.nytimes.com/2015/11/29/magazine/the-serial-swatter.html

22 Jaclyn Friedman, Anita Sarkeesian, and Renee Bracy Sherman, "Speak Up & Stay Safe(r): A Guide to Protecting Yourself from Online Harassment," Feminist Frequency, 2015. https://onlinesafety.feministfrequency.com/en/

23 Citron, 83.

24 *Ibid.*, 253.

4 Community: Cultivating a Circle of Solidarity

1 Amanda Hess, "Why Women Aren't Welcome on the Internet," first published 6 January 2014, updated 14 June 2017. https://psmag.com/social-justice/women-arent-welcome-internet-72170

2 Author interview with Talia Lavin, Virtual, 25 July 2021.

3 Statista, "Distribution of Twitter users worldwide as of April 2021, by gender," 2021. https://www.statista.com/statistics/828092/distribution-of-users-on-twitter-worldwide-gender/

4 Michael Barthel et al, "Reddit news users more likely to be male, young and digital in their news preferences," Pew Research Center, 25 February 2016. https://www.journalism.org/2016/02/25/reddit-news-users-more-likely-to-be-male-young-and-digital-in-their-news-preferences/

5 Chemaly, 157.

6 www.autoadmit.com

7   Ellen Nakashima, "Harsh Words Die Hard on the Web," *The Washington Post*, 7 March 2007. https://www.washingtonpost.com/wp-dyn/content/article/2007/03/06/AR2007030602705.html

8   Elizabeth Wurtzel, "Trash Talk," *The Wall Street Journal*, 19 March 2007. https://web.archive.org/web/20070323152741/http://www.opinionjournal.com/editorial/feature.html?id=110009805

9   Ian Sherr, "How to scrub hate off Facebook, Twitter and the internet," CNET, 27 November 2017. https://www.cnet.com/news/can-tech-fix-nazis-online-hate-harassment-facebook-twitter-trolls/

10 Author interview with Brittan Heller, Virtual, 1 July 2021.

11 Kelsey McKinney, Twitter post, 2 April 2021. https://web.archive.org/web/20210402153221/https://twitter.com/mckinneykelsey/status/1378007200799555590

12 Chemaly, 271.

5 Tenacity: Speaking Up and Fighting Back

1   Sheera Frenkel and Cecilia Kang, *An Ugly Truth*, (New York: Harper Collins, 2021). 8.

2   Ibid., 6.

3   Francesa Tripodi, "Ms. Categorized: Gender, notability, and inequality on Wikipedia," *New Media & Society*. June 2021. 1. https://journals.sagepub.com/doi/pdf/10.1177/14614448211023772

4   Ibid.

5   Ibid.

6   Nitasha Tiku, "Google hired Timnit Gebru to be an outspoken critic of unethical AI. Then she was fired for it.," *The Washington Post*, 23 December 2020. https://www.washingtonpost.com/technology/2020/12/23/google-timnit-gebru-ai-ethics/

7   Zoe Schiffer, "Timnit Gebru was Fired from Google—Then the Harassers Arrived," The Verge, 5 March 2021. https://www.theverge.com/22309962/timnit-gebru-google-harassment-campaign-jeff-dean

8   Ibid.

9   Katy Steinmetz, "She Coined the Term 'Intersectionality' Over 30 Years Ago. Here's What It Means to Her Today," TIME, 20 February 2020. https://time.com/5786710/kimberle-crenshaw-intersectionality/

10 UN Women, "Intersectional feminism: what it means and why it matters right now," UNWomen.org, 1 July 2020. https://www.unwomen.org/en/news/stories/2020/6/explainer-intersectional-feminism-what-it-means-and-why-it-matters

11 Wilson Center focus group with Shireen Mitchell et al, Virtual, 13 November 2020.

12 Jankowicz et al, 5, 42.

13 Maegan Parker Brooks and Davis W. Houck, The Speeches of Fannie Lou Hamer: To Tell It Like It Is, (Jackson: University Press of Mississippi, 2011), 134–139.

14 Chemaly, 151.

Index